GCSE ENGLISH 1

Reading & Understanding

RHODRI JONES

JOHN MURRAY

Acknowledgements

Copyright material is reproduced by kind permission of the copyright holders: Patricia W. Romero and Yale University Press (p. 7), Michael A. Pearson and Methuen (p. 7), Joe Corrie (p. 9), Joan Lingard and Hamish Hamilton (p. 9), *The Guardian* (pp. 9, 22, 32, 35, 67, 89), *Daily Express* (p. 11), Arnold Wesker and Cape (p. 11), Pedigree Petfoods Education Centre (p. 13), Lloyds Bank (p. 13), Jack London (p. 14), *The Sun* (pp. 14, 98), Margaret Drabble and Weidenfeld & Nicolson (p. 15), Parker Pens (p. 18), Equal Opportunities Commission (p. 19), *The Observer* (pp. 19, 62, 66), A & C Black ('St Albans', p. 21), *Evening Standard* (pp. 21, 47–9, 80, 93, 98), Yugotours (p. 22), Mundi Color Iberia (p. 24), Barbara Cartland and Rupert Crew Ltd (p. 25), *Daily Mirror* (pp. 26, 60, 98 and cover), Hamish Hamilton (p. 27), *Sunday Telegraph* (pp. 29, 31, 80), Marjorie Darke and Penguin Books (p. 30), *New Statesman* (p. 32), Chatto & Windus (p. 33), Andrew Rawnsley (p. 35), John Lehmann and Hogarth Press (from *Forty Poems*) (p. 35), Maud Gracechurch and Allen & Unwin (from *Never Rub Bottoms with a Porcupine*) (p. 38), Astor Cruises/Morgan Leisure Ltd (p. 39), Secondary Examinations Council, (p. 41), Dorothy M. Johnson and McIntosh and Otis, Inc. (p. 43), Ray Bradbury and Hart-Davies (from *The Golden Apples of the Sun* (p. 44), *Today* (p. 44), Next (p. 45), Prudential Property Services (p. 46), Roger Mais and Longman (from *Listen, the Wind*) (pp. 49–53), Martyn Sutton (p. 55), Malachi Whitacker and Carcanet Press (from *The Crystal Fountain*) (pp. 56–8), Times Newspapers Ltd 1986 and 1987 (TES 3.10.86 and 7.8.87) (p. 68, 103), Shirley Conran and Sidgwick & Jackson (p. 71), British Gas (p. 71) Controller of Her Majesty's Stationery Office (p. 72–3), Lynne Reid Banks and Chatto & Windus (p. 75), Edward Blishen and Hamish Hamilton (p. 75), Laurence Pollinger and the estate of Frieda Lawrence Ravagli (p. 76 and cover), Auberon Waugh (pp. 80, 86), Reginald Rose and ICM Inc. (pp. 82–3), Renault (p. 85), *London Daily News* (p. 87), Terry Jones (p. 89), Nance Lui Fyson and Batsford (p. 92), Geoffrey Paradise and Barnet Press (p. 95), *Mid Sussex Times* (p. 96), *The Independent* (p. 98 and cover), Oxford and Cambridge University Presses (p. 100), Crown Copyright (p. 101), Don McCullin and Metropolitan Police (pp. 104–5), Sir David McNee and Collins (p. 106), and the French Government Tourist Office, *Good Housekeeping*, Penguin Books and *Sky* (cover). Every effort has been made to trace copyright holders, but we will be pleased to rectify any omissions in future printings.

First published 1989
by John Murray (Publishers) Ltd
50 Albemarle St, London W1X 4BD

Cover illustration by
Sebastian Quigley/Linden Artists
Typeset by Phoenix Photosetting, Chatham
Printed and bound in Great Britain at
The Bath Press, Avon

British Library Cataloguing
in Publication Data

Jones, Rhodri
    GCSE English
    1: Reading and understanding
    1. English language. Reading –
    Questions & answers – For schools
    1. Title
    428.4'076

ISBN 0–7195–4666–4

Contents

Introduction

Reading and Understanding is the first book of *GCSE English*, a complete GCSE course. The other books are *Writing and Coursework* and *Oral Communication*.

In *Reading and Understanding*, you are guided through various activities, developing skills which it is necessary for you to acquire if you are to be able to read critically and with full understanding. These range from a study of the various kinds of language that writers use, to developing the ability to evaluate a point of view that is being presented.

A wide variety of writing is provided for you to examine and analyse – advertisements, newspaper reports and editorials, letters, extracts from novels, plays and short stories, poems and complete short stories, extracts from non-fiction books and travel brochures, examples of information leaflets and official documents. They illustrate the diverse uses to which the language is put and the vast range of printed material that you may encounter and be expected to cope with.

The skills required to read critically and the ability to respond to and evaluate all types of writing are what GCSE English examines. The advice given here and the practice suggested should help you to develop and demonstrate these skills and this ability, whether you sit an examination as part of your course or whether you are assessed solely on coursework.

This is not a book of comprehension passages and questions. Each section looks at a specific skill or aspect of reading and provides material which enables you to study this skill or aspect in detail. The book is divided into two parts. Part One is concerned with matters that affect an understanding of all writing. Part Two looks at more particular examples of types and uses of language. Some of the work requires a written response (your teacher may suggest this might be used as part of your coursework), but much of it may be done orally (your teacher may suggest you work in groups) and may provide an opportunity for oral assessment.

The book is based on a close examination of the National Grade Criteria and the syllabuses of all the GCSE examining groups.

Part One

Looking at General Aspects of Language

1 ❖ Kinds of Language

Consider the following statements. How would you describe the differences in the kind of language used in each?

Wot a geezer!

What a strange person!

There are many different kinds of language, depending on the words writers use and the way they are put together. Language can be simple, technical, obscure, scientific, babyish, offensive, hackneyed, formal, informal, and so on.

From a linguistic point of view, language can be divided into five broad categories – Standard English, colloquial English, slang, jargon and dialect.

Standard English

This is the language used by the majority of educated English-speaking people. It is formal in tone and grammatically 'correct'. It would be used in formal situations, for example, in business letters, reports, biographies, histories, textbooks, serious journalism. Here is an example:

> I first came upon Sylvia on a visit to Addis Ababa, Ethiopia. As a feminist, my imagination was caught by this English woman who loyally served the Ethiopian monarchy from the first days of the Italian invasion until her death in December 1960. On a visit to Trinity Cathedral, I was struck by her impressive tomb. She was the only foreigner buried in an area reserved for the patriots of the Italian war.
>
> *Patricia W. Romero*, E. SYLVIA PANKHURST, PORTRAIT OF A RADICAL

Colloquial English

This is freer and more relaxed than Standard English. It is the language used in everyday speech between friends and in informal situations. It uses idiomatic phrases called colloquialisms ('How are things?'), abbreviations ('I've' for 'I have') and need not necessarily be grammatically correct ('I feel real bad' instead of 'I feel really bad'). It would be used in letters to friends and relations, dialogue in plays and novels or narrative creating a relaxed tone of voice, popular journalism, some advertising. For example:

> Up till then the tennis had been a bit of an anti-climax. I'd been looking forward to it all afternoon. But once Jammy and I got on to the school tennis courts and started playing, I soon lost interest. We must be two of the worst players in the world, and even our McEnroe impressions weren't very good. However, when he told me that he was madly in love with Sharon I nearly died laughing.
>
> *Michael A. Pearson*, THE BUBBLE GUM CHAMPION

Slang

This is even further away from Standard English than colloquial language. (Compare Standard English 'drink', colloquial 'tipple' and slang 'booze'.) If colloquial language is 'friendly', then slang is 'matey'. Slang words can be regarded as vulgar in the wrong context. But it is possible for some slang words to become 'respectable' – for example, 'freezer', 'news flash' and 'zoom-lens' were recorded as slang in a dictionary of slang published in 1977. Slang expressions tend to be less widely used and understood than colloquial language. They also tend to be fashionable for a while and then become dated. Slang can be used to add liveliness or a sense of familiarity to writing, or can be used to shock or startle the reader. It can be found in some dialogue in plays and novels and in some popular journalism and advertising. For example:

Fingered – Grass named on shot gangster's wreath

Headline in DAILY MIRROR

GANGLAND PALS VOW TO NAIL THE SQUEALER

Headline in THE SUN

Jargon

This is the name given to specialised or technical language used among members of a particular group or profession which might be unintelligible to people outside that group or profession. For instance, a sociologist might use expressions like 'social system', 'institutionalisation', 'value-orientation', 'patterns of conformity', 'deviance', 'motivational processes'. Jargon can legitimately be used by one expert writing for others in scientific, technical and academic works, but it would not normally be suitable for the ordinary reader. Note, however, that many words which could be considered as jargon have come into common use. Examples can be found in the worlds of television, newspapers and pop music.

Dialect

This is the form of language peculiar to a particular area or social class. It is determined by such factors as where you live, your family background, employment and education. Different dialects are marked off from each other by differences in pronunciation, vocabulary and grammar – for example, the words 'bairns', 'weans' and 'childer' are dialectal forms found in different areas of Britain for 'children'. Dialect is found more commonly in speech, but it can be used in dialogue in plays and novels and in writing which seeks to emphasise a particular locality. The following extract is an example from a play set in Scotland.

AGNES: Is your mither in, Jenny?
JENNY: No, she's awa' doon the street, auntie . . . Sit doon.
          (AGNES sits at left of table.)
JENNY: What's a' the noise aboot the nicht?
AGNES: I dinna ken. There's been a meetin' in the hall aboot something.
          Oor Tam'll no' go to the meetin's to let us ken what's gaun on.

Joe Corrie, IN TIME O' STRIFE

Note:

1   It would be misleading to say that one of these kinds of language is 'right' and another 'wrong'. The kind of language used depends on the subject matter and the situation, the audience addressed and the purpose of the writing. (See chapters 2 and 5.)

2   Writers do not always keep to the same kind of language all the time in a piece of writing. For instance, in a story the writer is likely to use colloquial language in dialogue and Standard English for the narrative. For example:

> 'Labouring's well paid, Sadie, but it's a terrible job and I'm not wanting to do it for ever.'
> She had had plans for new curtains. She had seen material in the store that day and had measured up the window when Kevin was out. His face, which had been beaming when he came in, was now sobered.

Joan Lingard, INTO EXILE

An editorial in a quality newspaper might use a slang word in the middle of Standard English in order to surprise or amuse readers. For example:

> The May Day Bank Holiday, introduced by Michael Foot in his time at the Department of Employment as a national celebration of labour, looks set for the chop.

THE GUARDIAN

3   The English language is constantly changing. For instance, what may be regarded as slang one day may be perfectly acceptable in Standard English the next. See the examples given earlier under 'Slang'.

A Consider the various examples given above and say how effective each is as an illustration of a particular kind of language.

B Find further short passages which illustrate each of these kinds of language. You may find other examples in this book or from your own reading.

C Consider the following words and expressions. What kind of language does each belong to? What kind of written context might you find each of them in? Justify your view. There may be more than one possibility in some cases.

lady	use your loaf
tea-leaf	under the weather
mash	sweet
gasbag	well-oiled
hairy	shippen

D Find other words which refer to the same thing as each of the following. Say what kind of language each of your variants belongs to. In what written contexts might you find each of them?

money	die
lavatory	prison
police officer	wife
head	girl
man	

E Find examples of jargon originating in the newspaper world, television, pop music, psychology and sociology which have come into common use.

F If you know a dialect well, make a list of words and phrases from that dialect and give their Standard English equivalents.

G Say what kind of language the following passages are written in. Rewrite each of them in Standard English. What does your version lose or gain in each case?

Homely Arthur is a household hero

NO Place Like Home (BBC1 7.0 p.m.) finally got its act together with an episode which was actually funny.

For far too long, this series has had a cosy billet at peak times relying for its weak humour on half-witted children sponging off Mum and Dad.

However, in last night's show only three of the accursed brood made an appearance and the comedy relied instead on magnificent Arthur (William Gaunt) and his grown-up sidekicks.

DAILY EXPRESS

☐1

☐2

JENNY: What do Ronnie say to it?
BEATIE: He don't mind. He don't even know though. He ent never bin here. Not in the three years I known him. But I'll tell you [*she jumps up and moves around as she talks*] I used to read the comics he bought for his nephews and he used to get riled – [*Now* BEATIE *begins to quote Ronnie, and when she does she imitates him so well in both manner and intonation that in fact as the play progresses we see a picture of him through her.*] 'Christ, woman, what can they give you that you can be so absorbed?' So you know what I used to do? I used to get a copy of the *Manchester Guardian* and sit with that wide open – and a comic behind!
JIMMY: *Manchester Guardian?* Blimey Joe – he don' believe in hevin' much fun then?
BEATIE: That's what I used to tell him. 'Fun?' he say, 'fun? Playing an instrument is fun, painting is fun, reading a book is fun, talking with friends is fun – but a comic? A comic? for a young woman of twenty-two?'
JENNY [*handing out meal and sitting down herself*]: He sound a queer bor to me. Sit you down and eat, gal.
BEATIE: [*enthusiastically*]: He's alive, though.
JIMMY: Alive? Alive you say? What's alive about someone who can't read a comic? What's alive about a person that reads books and looks at paintings and listens to classical music? [*There is a silence at this, as though the question answers itself – reluctantly.*]

Arnold Wesker, ROOTS

2◆Appropriate Language

Consider the following statements:

It's about time people doing porridge had a decent shot of getting a bit of an education.

Prisoners ought to have greater opportunities to engage in educational activities.

What difference is there in the kind of language each uses? Which would be more likely to appear in an official report on prisons? Why? Which would be more appropriate in such a context?

For a piece of writing to be effective, the language used should be appropriate. It should be appropriate to the subject matter and the situation, the audience addressed, and the purpose of the writing.

If the **subject matter** and the **situation** are serious and factual, Standard English is likely to be the most appropriate kind of language, for example, in a government report, a letter to a council official, a history or a biography. If the subject matter and situation are more light-hearted, colloquial language may be more appropriate, for example, in a comic story, the gossip column in a newspaper, letters between friends.

If the **audience** is a general audience, unknown to the writer, then formal language is more appropriate. That is why most non-fiction books are written in Standard English. Where writers seek to be more familiar with their audience and treat them like friends, they may use less formal language (colloquial language, slang, dialect), for example, some journalism, some advertising, a novel where the narrator speaks directly to the reader.

If the **purpose** of the writing is to inform or convey information, then Standard English is probably more appropriate because this is the kind of language most universally understood. For other purposes (to amuse, persuade, shock), less formal language may be more suitable.

Another way of looking at it is to compare how people speak in different situations. Someone making a public address would probably speak more formally than when chatting with friends. It is the same with writing.

A What kind of language would you expect to find in the following situations? Justify your view.

1   An account of the causes of the First World War

2   A headteacher's report to the governors of the school

3   An advertisement for a new pop record

4 An autobiography by a former prime minister

5 A letter to *The Sun*

6 A letter to *The Times*

7 A guide to Paris

8 A newspaper article debunking the pleasures of Christmas in a humorous way

9 A play about a working-class family in the East End of London

10 A newspaper article about cruelty to children (specify the newspaper).

B Consider the following passages. Say whether the kind of language used is appropriate, as far as you can tell. Justify your view. Take into account the subject matter and situation, the audience addressed and the purpose of the writing.

1

HOLIDAYS

f you plan to put your dog or cat in kennels or a cattery whilst you are on holiday, book early, and try to visit the establishment in advance. Most boarding kennels will only take dogs or cats if vaccination certificates are up to date, so check this in good time.

If friends or neighbours are willing to look after your pet, make sure they are familiar with his needs, have an adequate supply of his regular food, and can give enough time to the job.

It is an offence under the Abandonment of Animals Act for an owner to abandon an animal, whether permanently or not, in circumstances likely to cause suffering.

If, at any time, you plan to take an animal abroad, discuss it with your veterinary surgeon. Under the Rabies Importation Order 1974, it is a serious offence to bring any animal into the United Kingdom without making the necessary quarantine arrangements in advance.

THE PET OWNERS' CODE OF CONDUCT

2

'Do you remember all the hoo-hah a couple of years back about free banking?

'Everyone thought, hallelujah, no more bank charges.

'Me, I didn't believe a word of it.

'Banks are businesses after all, not charities.

'And, as I was wont to say, "There's no such thing as a free lunch."

'Sorry if I sound a bit of a cynic. It's not one of my more endearing qualities, but it comes from working at P. J. Wright and Partners for so long.

'Indeed I'd spent the previous 6 years seemingly marooned in the Export/Import department.

'Still, I thought, with a bit of luck and a lot of work, promotion might just be in sight come September.

'My memory of the next 6 months was one of long hours and shortened weekends.

'So when our next wedding anniversary came around I decided it was high time to re-introduce myself to the lady I'd married. . .'

From an advertisement for LLOYDS BANK

3

Me? I'm not a drooler. I'm the assistant. I don't know what Miss Jones or Miss Kelsey could do without me. There are fifty-five low-grade droolers in this ward, and how could they ever all be fed if I wasn't around? I like to feed droolers. They don't make trouble. They can't. Something's wrong with most of their legs and arms, and they can't talk. They're very low-grade. I can walk, and talk, and do things. You must be careful with the droolers and not feed them too fast. Then they choke. Miss Jones says I'm an expert. When a new nurse comes I show her how to do it. It's funny watching a new nurse try to feed them. She goes at it so slow and careful that supper time would be around before she finished shoving down their breakfast. Then I show her, because I'm an expert. Dr Dalrymple says I am, and he ought to know. A drooler can eat twice as fast if you know how to make him.

My name's Tom. I'm twenty-eight years old. Everybody knows me in the institution. This is an institution, you know. It belongs to the State of California and is run by politics. I know. I've been here a long time. Everybody trusts me. I run errands all over the place, when I'm not busy with the droolers. I like droolers. It makes me think how lucky I am that I ain't a drooler.

Jack London, TOLD IN THE DROOLING WARD

4

SOZZLED SANTA'S CANTER

A SOZZLED Santa rested merry in the nick—after his horse-drawn sleigh ran into a startled motorist.

Brothers Steve and Dave Thould had gone ho ho ho in 20 pubs collecting for charity in Evesham, Worcs.

Furious

Seasonal well-wishers plied them with pint after pint of cider—and they trotted past a red light on the way home.

Police said Steve, 35, may be charged with "furious riding" and being drunk in charge of his horse, Cracker.

Dave, 38, said: "I don't remember much about it, but it was a good night."

THE SUN

5

She gazes at herself in wonder. Vanished are her healthy pink cheeks, her slightly red winter nose, her mole, her little freckles and blemishes: she is smooth, new made. She dabs a little powder on top, and stands back to admire the effect. It is pleasing, she decides. She wonders what it will look like by midnight. Will she be transformed into an uneven, red-faced, patchy, blotchy clown? An ugly sister? Alix has always felt rather sorry for the poor competitive disappointed Ugly Sisters. Indeed, she feels sorry for almost everybody. It is one of her weaknesses. But she does not feel sorry for her friend Liz Headleand. As she struggles into her blue dress, she wonders idly if she is so fond of Liz because she does not have to feel sorry for her, or if she does not have to feel sorry for her because she is so fond of her? Or are the two considerations quite distinct? She feels she is on the verge of some interesting illumination here, but has to abandon it in order to search for Brian, to ask him to fasten the back of her dress: if she does not leave soon, she will be late for her early arrival, and moreover she has promised to meet Esther Breuer at eight thirty precisely on the corner of Harley Street and Weymouth Street. They plan to effect a double entry.

Margaret Drabble, THE RADIANT WAY

3◆Kinds of Writing

Consider these statements:

> When the dog cringed and began to whimper, Mary spoke to it softly and stroked its head.

> The dog licence has been abolished.

> Buy your dog Rover Dog-Food – the dog-food all dogs love.

Comment on any differences you can find between these three statements. For instance, what do you think the purpose is behind each of them?

Writing can be divided into three categories – expressive writing, informative writing and persuasive writing.

Expressive writing is imaginative writing that appeals to the imagination, the feelings and the intellect – for example, novels, short stories, plays and poems.

Informative writing is writing that sets out to give the reader information – for example, newspaper reports, instruction manuals, guide books.

Persuasive writing is writing that sets out to influence your opinion and win you over to a particular point of view – for example, editorials in newspapers, advertisements, political pamphlets.

If you can distinguish between these three kinds of writing, it can help you to determine the purpose or intention behind the writing and so help you to evaluate it more objectively. For instance, some newspaper reports and advertisements try to pass themselves off as factual (that is, informative writing) when in reality they are mixing facts and opinions and trying to influence you (that is, persuasive writing).

Note: Some writing can be of more than one kind. An autobiography, for instance, may be both informative and expressive; a poem may be both expressive and persuasive.

A What kind of writing do you think each of the following is likely to be? In some cases, more than one kind of writing is possible.

   1   A magazine article about the use of make-up

   2   A newspaper report about an earthquake

3   A play about young unemployed people

4   A leaflet on child benefit issued by the DHSS

5   A newspaper article in a series entitled 'My Point of View'

6   A recipe for curried chicken

7   A novel about the suffragettes

8   Instructions on how to wire up a plug

9   An advertisement for Help the Aged

10 A report by a firm to its shareholders.

B Examine the following passages. What kind of writing would you say each is? Justify your view.

The crest of this terrible natural façade passed among the neighbouring inhabitants as being seven hundred feet above the water it overhung. It had been proved by actual measurement to be not a foot less than six hundred and fifty.

That is to say, it is nearly three times the height of Flamborough, half as high again as the South Foreland, a hundred feet higher than Beachy Head—the loftiest promontory on the east or south side of this island—twice the height of St Aldhelm's, thrice as high as the Lizard, and just double the height of St Bee's. One seaboard point on the western coast is known to surpass it in altitude, but only by a few feet. This is Great Orme's Head, in Caernarvonshire.

And it must be remembered that the cliff exhibits an intensifying feature which some of those are without—sheer perpendicularity from the half-tide level.

Thomas Hardy, A PAIR OF BLUE EYES

Little wonder they don't build cars like they used to. Building a pen is difficult enough.

Oh, the elegant lines of the 1925 Hispano Suiza. Oh, the elegant lines of the 1927 Parker Duofold.

The car may no longer be available but happily the pen is making a welcome return.

We have long yearned to recreate this favourite Parker design. And our approaching centenary has provided a suitable excuse.

Like today's top cars the Parker Duofold Centennial boasts working parts that are 'state-of-the-art'.

But unlike them, it boasts workmanship that is somewhat old fashioned.

Rather than mould the cap and barrel 'en masse', we machine them as we did in the old days, from a solid block.

Rather than cut the nib from some modern metal, we stay true to gold.

Rather than slit the nib on some new fangled contraption, we still do the job by hand, using a blade no thicker than a human hair.

And just as Hispano Suiza road tested its cars thoroughly after manufacture, we put our pens through their paces.

Upon completion, each Duofold Centennial is examined by a white-gloved inspector. If deemed perfect, it is filled, written with and cleaned before being released for sale.

It is an exhausting way to produce a pen. But, as with the Hispano Suiza, the looks and handling provide ample reward.

Advertisement for a PARKER *pen*

3

Choosing a Career

You probably have one or two ideas in mind already. But beware! Don't limit your choice . . . . . .

Don't think in terms of boys' careers or girls' careers. There are no such things.

Boys with the right qualifications and qualities can now do many jobs that were closed to them before by tradition. Yet many boys could do them well and enjoy them. Young men are already finding satisfactory employment in *nursing, hairdressing, cookery, art, secretarial work* (leading on to the use of computer-based equipment) *or social work.*

Girls will find that careers open to them have increased enormously. With the right qualifications and qualities they can consider, for example, *accountancy, engineering, marketing, management* and a wide range of jobs in *building and construction*. Jobs in the medical profession including *anaesthetist, surgeon, dentist, optician* – in addition to the more traditional nursing.

Girls must not be automatically barred from tackling heavy manual work. If they have the strength they can be considered for the job.

Equal Opportunities Commission,
WIDER HORIZONS

4

There was a young man from Peru
Who believed that a secret he knew.
The secret was flight,
So he flew like a kite,
And now he's star turn in a zoo.

Barry (15)

5

The arrogance of the advertiser knows no barriers. We now have to pay the price of a paperback book for a catalogue from Harrods or Laura Ashley, to look at pictures of goods which they want to sell us at a very large profit. I understand that they are looking into ways of making us pay for looking at their newspaper ads as well, through sealing some of the pages which could only be opened by inserting a 50 pence coin.

Ads on hoardings present more difficulties: it might be necessary to institute random checks, with a system of spot fines for people found studying an advertising display for nothing. Television ads are easy. We could all contribute to a special levy, the proceeds to be distributed among all advertisers on ITV. That way, at least, they wouldn't be out of pocket. God forbid that the consumer should escape having to stump up to be persuaded to spend some more of his money.

Marcel Berlins,
THE OBSERVER MAGAZINE

C Find other examples of expressive, informative and persuasive writing. You could use other passages in this book or from your own reading.

4◆Tone

Look at the following statements:

A fine mess you've got me into!

This is an absolutely splendid achievement.

If these statements were spoken, how would you describe the kind of tone of voice likely to be used in each?

In speech, the tone in which words are spoken can vary considerably. It could be pleasant, unpleasant, grudging, sarcastic, innocent, devious, absent-minded, casual, envious, arrogant, and so on. The tone used in different pieces of writing can also vary considerably. Some pieces of writing can be neutral (as in instructions and explanations), but others can be described as passionate, offensive, sincere, enthusiastic, defiant, ingratiating, blunt, aggressive, resentful, and so on.

The tone of a piece of writing reveals the writer's attitude to the subject and the audience. It can be detected by examining:

the **words** the writer uses (calling a pet mongrel 'a noble hound' or 'a lovable mutt' or 'a miserable cur')

the **kind of language used** (the degree of formality or informality)

the **general approach** to the subject and the audience (sympathetic or unsympathetic, serious or frivolous, distant or familiar).

By using a tone that is appropriate, writers can reinforce the effectiveness of what they say. It is important too for readers to recognise the tone being used. If they fail to do so, there is a danger that they may misunderstand or misinterpret a piece of writing (for example, a piece that is ironic may be taken at face value).

A What tone would you expect a writer to use in each of the following? Justify your view. Several different tones may be appropriate in some instances.

1 An account of how to prune apple trees

2 A poem about the death of a child

3 An editorial in favour of capital punishment

4 A letter applying for a job

5 An advertisement for a film

6 A letter to the council about delays in refuse collection

7 A personal account of being bullied at school

8 A description for a guidebook of the White Cliffs of Dover

9 A story about someone falling in love

10 A newspaper report of a major road accident (specify the newspaper).

B Examine the following passages. What kind of tone is the writer using in each? How can you tell? Is the choice of tone appropriate as far as you can judge?

1

Most of the other monastic buildings were destroyed after the Reformation but the *Abbey Gatehouse* (1361), now part of St Albans School, survives a few yards W of the cathedral. Abbey Lane leads down to a bridge over the Ver, near the little *Fighting Cocks Inn*, probably on the site of a boathouse of the Saxon monastery.

'St Albans' *in* THE BLUE GUIDE TO ENGLAND

2

I cannot but conclude the bulk of your natives to be the most pernicious race of little odious vermin that nature ever suffered to crawl upon the surface of the earth.

Jonathan Swift, GULLIVER'S TRAVELS

3

□ I AM a London taxi driver and I do resent your headline "Don't be left standing by the cabbies". All the good work we do seems to go unnoticed; for instance my own circuit raised £15,000 for Children in Need. Not a mention of this was in any of the papers. We don't expect publicity for that. We don't expect publicity when we take old age pensioners or nurses home free of charge. But as soon as someone gets left standing on the kerb by a cabbie it is headlines in your paper. Do you think this is fair?

Letter in EVENING STANDARD

> *Enjoy even greater value with our incredible off-peak prices!*
> *This is a really fantastic opportunity for those lucky enough to take their holiday out of the high-season period. We are offering holidays taken before 18th May and after 22nd September at amazingly low prices, that mean even greater value for money.*
> *There are some terrific bargains to be had – and you'll really be able to enjoy the best of both worlds, as Yugoslavia is a delight all year round. Enjoy the country's beauty and tranquillity to the full . . . And of course, the weather is still glorious.*
> *Look out for Yugotours Superdeals – for prices you won't believe.*
>
> From YUGOTOURS *summer holiday brochure*

4

5

The Grand Knockout Tournament

'Savour again the delights of these zany games,' it says here in the hopeful tone of someone offering you turkey vol au vents on the 12th day of Christmas. A mercifully edited version of the joust-a-minute charity do in which the younger royals and celebrity courtiers did silly things for charity.

TV Briefing in THE GUARDIAN

6

O! She doth teach the torches to burn bright.
It seems she hangs upon the cheek of night
Like a rich jewel in an Ethiop's ear;
Beauty too rich for use, for earth too dear.

William Shakespeare, ROMEO AND JULIET

C Find three pieces of writing each of which is expressed in a different tone. You may choose from other extracts in this book or from your own reading.

5 ◆ Audience Addressed

Stand out in a crowd in X Brand jeans

What audience or reader do you think that advertising slogan is intended to appeal to?

Presumably, it is meant to appeal to people who want to stand out in a crowd, who want to be noticed and who want to be considered special or different.

Some writers claim that they write only for themselves. They are concerned to say what they want to say and get it right, and if no one else wishes to read it, then that is irrelevant. But most pieces of writing have a particular audience in mind.

A striking example is **advertising**. Where a particular product (for example, clothes, records, films, holidays) appeals to a particular type of person (for example, young, affluent, discriminating, elderly), then the advertisements direct what they say and how they say it in that direction. In fact, advertisers use appeals to many different emotions and attitudes to reach their audience – for example, vanity, fear, sex, keeping up with famous people, a sense of superiority and exclusiveness, envy, comedy, sentimentality.

Another area where the audience is especially important is **journalism**. Particular newspapers have particular readers, and the way news and opinion are presented takes this fact into account. Newspapers are commonly divided into two categories – the quality press and the tabloid press (alternative descriptions are 'serious' and 'popular'). Quality newspapers are concerned with covering the most important events at home and abroad in some detail, together with articles commenting on these events. They cater for readers who want to know what is going on and who want to think about the issues involved. Tabloid newspapers concentrate more on 'human interest' stories, on sensational and scandalous events, and on news of the affairs of 'celebrities'. They provide less detail, are written in a simpler style, and set out to entertain as much as to inform. *The Times* is regarded as a quality newspaper while the *Sun* is a tabloid. Newspapers like the *Daily Mail* are in between. Newspapers also generally reflect the particular political views of their readers.

In the world of **fiction**, where writers are working in a particular genre (for example, romances, science fiction, thrillers), they will tailor what they write to meet the expectations of their audience. In **non-fiction**, writers have to decide whether they are writing for people with experience of their subject or for beginners, and adapt their approach and language accordingly.

Working out the audience a writer is addressing in a particular piece of writing can help you to weigh up how effective the writing is. For instance, it would be unfair to criticise a writer for using simple language if the story is intended for 5-year-old children.

Similarly, it can help you to weigh up whether the writer is addressing the audience in a fair and legitimate way. Some advertising, some fiction and some journalism use dubious methods and appeal to the baser or weaker elements in human nature.

To work out the audience a writer is addressing, you should examine:

– the subject matter and treatment

– the language used

– the tone

– the particular appeal.

A Find examples of advertisements that appeal to vanity, fear, sex, keeping up with famous people, a sense of superiority and exclusiveness, envy, comedy, sentimentality.

B Collect advertisements dealing with a particular subject (for example, cars, holidays, cosmetics, cigarettes) and discuss the kinds of appeal the advertisers use.

C List all the national daily and Sunday newspapers. Arrange them into quality and tabloid and 'in between'. Find out and state the political slant that each of them has.

D Compare a quality newspaper with a tabloid newspaper and consider the audience each is intended for. Look at the main news stories in each, how home and international news is covered, the language and tone, the way pictures are used, and so on.

E Consider the particular appeal of each of the following – romances, westerns, thrillers, science fiction, crime stories. What elements would you expect a writer to include in each?

F Examine the following passages. What kind of audience do you think each is aimed at? How can you tell?

1

Recent years have seen enormous changes in holiday patterns. Large concentrations of people in the same old expanding places have become the norm.
Individuality, Reliability, Flexibility and Authenticity have all been sacrificed in the urge to get everyone to do the same as everyone else.
At Mundi Color we believe your holiday is an individual affair. We don't "send" large numbers of people anywhere.
When you travel with Mundi Color the only person on the aircraft who knows you are a Mundi Color client . . . is you!

From Mundi Color Iberia summer holiday brochure

A long time later when the fire was only a golden glow and the flames had died down, the Marquess said:

"I wish there were words in which I could tell you what it means to be here with you in my own home, on my own land, surrounded by the people who love and respect me and whom I will serve so long as I live."

"That is just how I want you to think," Arina answered.

He drew her closer to him feeling the softness of her body, and knowing that only to touch her was to be aware he touched the perfection he had always sought in a woman.

"How can I have been so lucky to have found you?" he asked.

"I am sure you will think it is a . . . strange thing to say, but it was Papa who helped me when I was so . . . desperate and who sent me first to Lady Beverley and in some magical way arranged that you should overhear my conversation with her."

Arina paused. Then she said:

"Only a man with the real instincts of kindness could have helped me as you did."

"It was not only your father, but your prayers, my darling, which told me what to do."

As the Marquess spoke he thought it was a strange thing for him to say and believe.

Yet he had known ever since his return to the Castle that the supercilious cynicism that had governed the way he thought and talked with his friends at White's and with the women who came and went in his life had vanished.

But now he thought to himself, it was impossible in Scotland to be anything but honest.

He knew that just as Arina had anticipated that the beauty of the Castle and the moors would lift his mind from everything that was small and petty, they had in fact made him bigger in himself than he had ever been in the past.

Now, for the first time, he could understand his father's air of omnipotence, and his desire not only for the greatness of the Clan, but also for the greatness of Scotland.

He turned his head to look down at Arina and thought in the light of the dying fire that nobody could look more lovely or more spiritual, and that she was different from every other woman he had ever known.

He could see her eyes looking at him adoringly and he told himself he would never fail her and that he vowed in the future to live up to her ideals.

Barbara Cartland, THE CALL OF THE HIGHLANDS

THE RAT IS BACK

★ THE terrible Turk is back — and he's still up to his wicked tricks. Smoothie Mehmet Osman slips into Albert Square again tomorrow (EASTENDERS omnibus edition, BBC-1, 2.0) to wreak fresh havoc.

"Oh, yes, he's still a gambler and womaniser. Nothing changes," says actor Haluk Bilginer, who plays the Romeo rat.

"But he's not an evil person. It's just that he's a total gambler with life and gets himself in situations where he is judged as a nasty piece of work."

Mehmet seems to appeal to the ladies all right.

Once a car full of amorous young women were responsible for him being nicked by police and ending up in court.

"Yes, it's absolutely true," says the 33-year-old actor.

"I was driving in North London when a car drew alongside me and all these women inside recognised me and started yelling at me.

"I decided the only thing to do was get rid of them, so I put my foot down and the next thing I knew the boys in blue were on my tail."

They clocked him doing 79 mph in a 50 mph area, didn't think much of his story — and booked him for speeding.

The magistrates were apparently not fans of Mehmet either. They fined Haluk £75 and gave him three penalty points.

PAULINE McLEOD

DAILY MIRROR

3

4

A silence followed. I listened to the rain lashing the windows. The smell of cigarette smoke came through the crack of the door. I wanted to cough. I bit hard on a handkerchief.

The purring voice said, still gentle: 'From what I hear this blonde broad was just a shill for Geiger. I'll talk it over with Eddie. How much you tap the peeper for?'

'Two centuries.'

'Get it?'

Harry Jones laughed again. 'I'm seeing him to-morrow. I have hopes.'

'Where's Agnes?'

'Listen——'

'Where's Agnes?'

Silence.

'Look at it, little man.'

I didn't move. I wasn't wearing a gun. I didn't have to see through the crack of the door to know that a gun was what the purring voice was inviting Harry Jones to look at. But I didn't think Mr Canino would do anything with his gun beyond showing it. I waited.

'I'm looking at it,' Harry Jones said, his voice squeezed tight as if it could hardly get past his teeth. 'And I don't see anything I didn't see before. Go ahead and blast and see what it gets you.'

'A Chicago overcoat is what it would get you, little man.'

Raymond Chandler, THE BIG SLEEP

6 ◆ The Colour of Words

Compare the following statements:

The smell was everywhere.

The perfume filled the air.

The stench was overpowering.

All three are saying more or less the same thing, but because of the words used, each has a particular bias. The first is neutral, the second is favourable, and the third is unfavourable.

Writers use words with a particular colour or bias to indicate to the reader that a situation or a character being described is meant to be pleasant or unpleasant, sympathetic or unsympathetic, and so on. For instance, compare the following:

He smiled at her reply.

He sneered at her reply.

He smirked at her reply.

Choosing words with a particular colour or bias can also reveal the attitude writers have towards their subjects, for example:

The police firmly pushed the crowd back.

The police brutally beat the crowd back.

In expressive writing, it is part of the writer's skill to choose words of the right colour or bias so that the impression the writer wants to give is clearly conveyed to the reader. But in persuasive writing, and even in some informative writing, writers sometimes choose words with a particular colour or bias in order to influence their readers rather than to present them with a neutral, factual account. For instance, the examples given above about the police might have come from two different accounts of the same event, but they give very different impressions. Unless the reader happened to be present, it would be impossible to say which is the more accurate version and which presents a biased view. With this kind of writing, readers need to be on their guard and have to weigh up the kind of words being used.

Another instance of how words can be coloured is the **euphemism**. This is the use of a milder word or phrase in place of one that could be considered objectionable or too explicit. For example, saying 'he has passed away' instead of 'he has died'. This may be justified sometimes in trying to soften the effect of what is said out of consideration for people's feelings. But often euphemisms are used to disguise the true facts. For instance, bombing raids have been described as 'air support', an invasion as 'a rescue mission', and telling a lie as 'being economical with the truth'.

A   Find words similar in meaning to each of the following. Say what colour or bias is present in each of your alternatives.

eat	big
speak	thin
ask	a wind
a sound	rain
small	a meal

B   Give the 'harsher' equivalents of the following euphemisms. In each case, say whether you think the use of the euphemism could be justified.

rodent officer	pacification
senior citizens	border realignment
outsize	adult videos
cloakroom	separate development
economy–size	posterior

Find other examples of euphemisms.

C   Write two postcards that someone on holiday might write to two different people. In the first, describe the holiday in glowing terms. In the second, describe the sordid reality.

D   Examine the following passages. Consider the particular colour or bias of the words being used or quoted in each. Say whether you think such words are being used fairly or unfairly, as far as you can tell.

This is not due to television. It is not due to social developments outside our control. It is not due to lack of resources. It is not due to unemployment, Thatcherism or anything else of that order. It is due to a false educational orthodoxy which argues that teaching the young to speak correctly is somehow an élitist conspiracy aimed at castrating the masses of their proletarian or ethnic creativity and verbal spontaneity. Not teaching them to speak correctly, therefore, becomes an act of liberation. So, thanks to HM Inspectorate, the people of England, who have not spoken yet, will now never be able to do so, except in sounds so raw and rough as to be comprehensible only in the animal kingdom long accustomed to roars, grunts and screeches.

Peregrine Worsthorne, THE SUNDAY TELEGRAPH

2. 'Hi . . . Gail! Gai-yul . . . hang about!'

On the right side of the open gates – the free world side – Gail paused. School din was already in her ears even before the shout. The prospect of all the rest was beginning to close over her head. A long list.

Chalk dust
Sweat stink
Old cabbage
Teachers
Boredom

Questions questions . . . hovering already.

She hadn't wanted to go in at all; was still struggling with the astonishment of getting this far. But the shout, loaded with questions to come, made her wish fervently that she could be at the top of the drive. She knew who was shouting, although the familiar voice sounded strangely different, like everything else. First day of term. Kids flocking in. The drive winding up the hill, through banks of grass and trees dividing the sunlight, to the concrete parking space at the top. Bike sheds filling. Everything the same. Everything different.

Reluctantly she turned and saw Heather Stafford ploughing up the slope of the road. Her freckled face glowed strawberry from running and the early September heat.

Chocolate flake on pink blancmange, Gail thought. Thick bare legs pink too. Sandy hair springing out like always. Big grin. In one hand a new school bag. Sprauncy oatmeal canvas and leather affair with tassels hanging from the strap. She felt a sudden total disgust for her own tatty ex-army haversack, once treasured.

'Dead keen, aren't you?' Heather panted. 'I've been trying to catch up ever since the bus stop. Where've you *been*? There's a rumour going round you had an accident. Run over or something. That true?'

Gail stared. 'Who said so?'

'Cathy Thomas.'

'She's nuts!'

'So it isn't true?'

The strangeness that had been following her around for weeks, now increased. 'Do I look mangled?'

'Can't say you do.'

'Well then!'

Heather examined her with dark seal-brown eyes. Long ago when they first arrived very new and nervous at Broadhayes Comprehensive, Gail had decided those eyes were a big con. Nothing had made her change that opinion. They ought to belong to a dreamy filmstar figure. Someone sad and romantic. Instead, built round those gorgeous melting eyes was this plump creature, full of bounce and chat. Blessed with a giggle like unplugged bathwater, and about as secret and full of Eastern Promise as an underdone sausage!

Marjorie Darke, COMEBACK

3

GOODBYE TO ALL BLACK

THE WELCOME RETURN OF SOFT BROWNS

Brown is back – subtle, dreamy shades that flatter the English complexion and look good in city cafés or country lanes. Colours come straight from a chocolate-box – truffle, caramel, toffee, cinnamon – and blend beautifully with misty autumnal greys. There are wrap-over bolero tops, loose swirling skirts and fluid trouser-suits in warm jerseys: milk, dark and cream chocolate tones blend together in soft woollen fabrics. Wear a grey cashmere dress with a hazel-coloured jacket (think of all the shades of the autumn countryside) or add some contrast to a truffle-coloured suit with a cream polo-neck (think of café-au-lait). Shop windows will be like a childhood fantasy of delicious delights: faced with this choice, all you have to do is open the chocolate box, dip in your fingers and indulge yourself in your favourite treats.

TELEGRAPH SUNDAY MAGAZINE

4

Rewriting the map in terms of television programmes and romantic writers enables the agent to conjure up glorious landscapes and idylls without having to be too specific.

Unattractive places can be glossed over; whole counties can disappear if necessary. Essex, for example, can be neatly disposed of as 'Constable country'. The Black Country becomes 'Arnold Bennett country'; the whole of metropolitan Tyneside becomes 'Catherine Cookson country'.

• • • • •

People who have been frequently exposed to estate agents' blurb soon learn to spot the creative geography. 'Hard by', 'overlooking', 'fringing' and 'bordering on' all mean the same thing – nowhere near. 'View of the river' does not mean with the naked eye, unless specified. 'Within a few minutes' stroll' tells you to take a knapsack and a stout stick. 'Main road within easy reach' means the M25 is at the bottom of the garden.

Christine Whelan,
TELEGRAPH SUNDAY MAGAZINE

7◆*Figurative Language*

Figurative language, when effectively used, can enliven a piece of writing and can present the reader with a more vivid impression of the writer's meaning. The main devices used in figurative writing are the metaphor and the simile.

The **metaphor** is a comparison in which one thing is said to be another which is not literally the case. For example:

Brian really is a clown.

Unless Brian performs in a circus, this is a figurative statement. What it does is make a comparison between Brian and a clown. By stating that Brian is a clown, it is making the point that Brian shares certain qualities or certain kinds of behaviour with a clown, for example, comic antics.

A **simile** is a comparison in which one thing is said to be like another. For example:

Brian is behaving like a clown.

Both of these examples are more interesting than the plain statement 'Brian is behaving in a silly way'. They enable the reader to measure Brian's behaviour against that of a clown and to gauge Brian's behaviour more clearly and precisely. The reader is given a picture of how Brian is behaving.

As well as making an idea clearer, figurative language can surprise the reader and present things in a fresh and unexpected way. It can draw parallels which the reader may not have thought of before. It can add to comic or dramatic effect. For example:

Yugoslavia, said Mel Brooks, is a country run on a 40-watt bulb.

TV Review in THE GUARDIAN

The language we use is full of metaphors which we are so used to that we no longer notice them – 'the heart of a problem', 'the feet of a table', 'a striking idea', 'a sinking feeling'. These are called **dead metaphors**.

Sometimes writers get carried away (another example of a dead metaphor) and overuse figurative language so that the effect becomes too rich or affected. For example:

Biliously, doubting that it ought to have risen, the sun hoisted itself over the horizon, its red-rimmed rays glinting nervously on the brazen rooftops of Czeskordzeny Racs.

Samuel McCracken in a NEW STATESMAN *parody*

Another danger of using too many metaphors is that one metaphor can follow too closely on another, and an incongruous and unintentionally humorous effect can be created. These are known as **mixed metaphors**. For example:

He is sitting on the fence and burying his head in the sand.

Sometimes writers use metaphors or similes that are inappropriate, again resulting in a ludicrous effect. For example:

Smith's knee is still giving the Arsenal manager a headache.

Writers can also use figurative language that is stale and hackneyed instead of searching for a more interesting or meaningful way of saying what they want to say. Examples of faded figurative language of this kind are 'to plough a lonely furrow', 'to nip something in the bud', 'as green as grass', 'as bright as a button', 'like something the cat brought in'. More examples are given in Chapter 8.

A   Comment on the effectiveness – or otherwise – of the following metaphors and similes, all taken from *Sunset at Blandings*, a comic novel by P. G. Wodehouse.

1   Sir James Piper, England's Chancellor of the Exchequer, sat in his London study staring before him with what one usually called unseeing eyes and snorting every now and then like somebody bursting a series of small paper bags.

2   Gally gazed at her, concerned. Beach, that shrewd diagnostician, had been right, he felt, though his 'somewhat depressed' had been an understatement. Here was plainly a niece whose soul had been passed through the wringer, a niece who had drained the bitter cup and, what is more, had found a dead mouse at the bottom of it.

3   Sir James was looking as an investor in some company might have looked on learning that its managing director had left England without stopping to pack.

4   'You may feel like Mary with her lamb, though I doubt whether anyone attached to Scotland Yard has fleece as white as snow.'

5   Jeff was in the corridor, warming up after his session with the Snow Queen.

B   Comment on the meaning and effectiveness of the figurative language used in these extracts from poems.

1   Somewhere in myself
        Pride, like a goldfish, flashed a sudden fin.

Edward Lucie-Smith, THE LESSON

2   The five never moved.
They just stood sucked empty
As grasses by this island's silence.

Ted Hughes, THE RESCUE

3 When the white feet of the baby beat across the grass
The little white feet nod like white flowers in a wind.

D. H. Lawrence, BABY RUNNING BAREFOOT

4 She said my father had whiskers and looked like God;
that he swore like a fettler, drank like a bottle.

Ray Mathew, OUR FATHER

5 Sun is torn in coloured petals on the water,
the water shivering in the heat and the north wind.

Rex Warner, NILE FISHERMEN

6 It moved so slowly, friendly as a dog
Whose teeth would never bite.

Vernon Scannell, A DAY ON THE RIVER

7 The parrots shriek as if they were on fire.

Ted Hughes, THE JAGUAR

8 The lunch hour: the shops empty, shopgirls' faces relax
Diaphanous as green glass, empty as old almanacs.

Louis MacNeice, BIRMINGHAM

9 The policeman stands on a plate of dirty light –
Statue of liberty, angel with flaming sword
As the whim takes him.

Norman MacCaig, TRAFFIC STOP

10 Oh as I was young and easy in the mercy of his means,
  Time held me green and dying
Though I sang in my chains like the sea.

Dylan Thomas, FERN HILL

C Comment on the figurative language in this account of Prime Minister's Question Time in the House of Commons.

KINNOCK POPS THE $1M QUESTION

"MR Speaker, what is the matter with this woman?" demanded Neil Kinnock during questions to the Prime Minister.

Once again Mr Speaker Weatherill was being cast into the unwelcome role of Parliament's agony uncle, the Claire Rayner of the Commons. He does not relish the part, indeed he does not want it at all.

"I have no idea what motives are in the minds of members when they speak," the Speaker explained yesterday. It is enough to have to deal with the rich assortment of clients who confront him every day, without having to put labels to their conditions.

Still, they persist. Mr Kinnock, a regular correspondent, is getting desperate. The Kinnock-Thatcher relationship is going through one of its stormier passages.

They spent Christmas and the New Year apart. Now they are back together again. Things have not improved. Absence has only made the heart grow harder.

They were never a well-matched pair. Mrs Thatcher has been through two other partners already. Mr Kinnock, in the rather chauvinistic way of men from the Welsh Valleys, has always resented the fact that Mrs Thatcher has a job, particularly when it is the job he wants.

As with a lot of couples who have been together for some time, most of the rows are about children. Desperate delays in operations, he shouts across at her. Enormous increases in the numbers of babies saved, she shouts back to him.

Then things get violent.

Andrew Rawnsley, THE GUARDIAN

D Comment on the imagery used in this poem.

To Penetrate that Room

To penetrate that room is my desire,
The extreme attic of the mind, that lies
Just beyond the last bend in the corridor.
Writing I do it. Phrases, poems are keys.
Loving's another way (but not so sure).
A fire's in there, I think, there's truth at last
Deep in a lumber chest. Sometimes I'm near,
But draughts puff out the matches and I'm lost.
Sometimes I'm lucky, find a key to turn,
Open an inch or two—but always then
A bell rings, someone calls, or cries of 'fire'
Arrest my hand when nothing's known or seen,
And running down the stairs again I mourn.

John Lehmann

E Find five metaphors and five similes from your own reading that you consider particularly effective.

8 ◆ Stale Language

Writers do not always search for new, fresh and original ways of saying things. Sometimes they use the first words that come to mind with the result that what they write is hackneyed and tired. Some types of stale language used in this way are clichés, officialese, faded figurative language, inevitable adjectives and vogue words.

Clichés

Clichés are idioms which are so overused and familiar that they have lost any freshness or originality they might once have had. For example, 'the calm before the storm', 'over the moon', 'when all is said and done', 'to keep a low profile', 'at the drop of a hat'.

Officialese

This is the kind of jargon (see Chapter 1) often found in writing by bureaucrats, politicians and advertisers where something simple is expressed in a roundabout and pompous way – for example, 'A review of the available facts by the department concerned has determined that . . .'

Faded figurative language

This consists of metaphors and similes so commonly used that they have lost any element of surprise or meaning. They are kinds of clichés. Examples are 'to turn over a new leaf', 'to leave no stone unturned', 'as cool as a cucumber', 'flat as a pancake', 'sick as a parrot'.

Inevitable adjectives

These are often used by journalists and advertisers. Certain nouns are always accompanied by the same adjectives so that the two words come as a ready-made phrase requiring no thought. For example, 'brutal murder', 'hard facts', 'agonising reappraisal', 'a perfect gentleman', 'pitched battle', 'dazzling smile'.

Vogue words

These are expressions which suddenly become fashionable and so become overused. They are sometimes used in an attempt to appear 'trendy' (itself a vogue word) or because they present an easy and lazy way of conveying an idea. Examples are 'status symbol', 'upmarket', 'an on-going situation', 'yuppie', 'the flavour of the month'.

A Comment on the effectiveness – or otherwise – of the language used in the following extracts from newspaper reports on football matches. Consider especially whether the figurative language used is stale or fresh.

1 It all started to go right for Tottenham manager Terry Venables yesterday but the agony goes on for Watford's Dave Bassett.

TODAY

2 High-flying Colchester came down to earth with a bump as they surrendered the Fourth Division leadership.

TODAY

3 Referee John Martin almost stole the limelight in this bruising battle yesterday before being upstaged by Swindon substitute Steve White.

TODAY

4 Newcastle's brilliant schemer Paul Gascoigne and Brazilian scoring ace Mirandinha yesterday virtually turned the League Championship into a one-horse race.

TODAY

5 Paul Moran launched the New Year for Tottenham on a rosy glow of optimism with a goal that blew a fanfare for the next generation of White Hart Lane kids.

THE STAR

6 Plymouth boss Dave Smith refused to make excuses after Reading tore up the form book with another shock away win.

THE STAR

7 Rampant Arsenal roared to their second impressive win in five days.

THE STAR

8 Liverpool's Dream Machine has become a colossal nightmare for the mere mortals who make up the rest of the First Division.

THE STAR

9 Nottingham Forest's championship hopes were gunned down by brilliant goals from Paul Gascoigne and Brazilian ace Mirandinha.

DAILY MIRROR

10 Chelsea's crisis deepened yesterday with frustrated fans again calling for the head of manager John Hollins.

DAILY MIRROR

11 Kevin Drinkell put himself in the shop window in spectacular style as the Norwich bandwagon rolled on.

DAILY MIRROR

12 From 25 yards Callaghan curled the ball round and over Wimbledon's wall to leave goalkeeper Dave Beasant rooted to his line.

DAILY MIRROR

B Comment on the language used in the following. It is a parody of a poem by Patience Strong.

GOD GIVE ME PATIENCE
A famous figure revived

To help us on life's busy road, a road both steep and long, a draught so fine that will revive is cordial Patience Strong. Too long has she rejected been, too long bethought as square; now of her splendid poesy have we become aware. For we've re-found her noble verse, re-learnt her wisdom fine, her genteel way of saving space, and her language, rich as wine. Her verses show life's weft and woof, both in sunshine and in showers, the sparkling dew upon the grass, the birds and bees and flowers. O, let us now praise Penguin books, who offer us this crown, this diadem of priceless pearls, as light as thistledown. So let's in triumph glasses raise and hymn in happy song the poets of great England's prime: Will Shakespeare and Miss Strong.

Maud Gracechurch

C Comment on the effectiveness – or otherwise – of the language used in the following advertisements. Look particularly at the adjectives used.

This is the Maiden Voyage of the world's newest luxury liner cruising regularly from Britain. [1]

On 2nd February 1987, *Astor* will sail away from a wintry Southampton into the glorious sunshine of the Caribbean, South America, the Ivory Coast, North Africa and through the Mediterranean to Genoa.

The highlight will be a 12-day adventure taking her 1,000 miles up the Amazon to Manaus and back.

As the untamed beauty of the Amazon slips by, you'll be able to enjoy *Astor's* superb five star cuisine, sophisticated entertainment and the sheer luxury of her lounges, suites and cabins.

And with no more than 600 international passengers, you'll always find plenty of space on *Astor* for quiet contemplation of some of the world's most breathtaking scenery.

You can take *Astor's* Maiden Voyage for the full 10 weeks from £4,730, or fly out and join her for shorter cruise options from only £1,200, including many free *Astor* extras.

Advertisement for ASTOR CRUISES

2

NEW INSTRUCTION
Who'll lend me £90,000 to buy this fantastic 3-bed. town house, I'm not telling anyone about its integral garage, prime location and spacious accommodation, so if you have this kind of money lying around lend it to me and we'll split the money in 2 years' time 60–40 in my favour, but don't tell anyone else that its only
£87,950

NEW INSTRUCTION
2-bed. house in private road, immaculate through-out, c.h., garage, second-ary double glazing, close to town centre, walking dis-tance to station, don't be a prune, view it today.

NEW INSTRUCTION
3-bed. semi-detached property. RURAL LOCA-TION, great accommo-dation, massive plot, backs onto open country, don't miss this golden oppor-tunity, 5 mins to M25, A1(M), 10 mins M1, can't find a better location.
OIRO £93,000

NEW INSTRUCTION
5-bed. extended palace, 3 regal receptions, 2 beautiful bathrooms, no expense spared, detached garage, good sized gardens, gas c.h., you'll never get another chance of luxury such as this.
£115,000

NEW INSTRUCTION
3-bed. semi in prime loca-tion, gas c.h., d/glazing, 90′ rear garden, why are we feeling so generous, hung over from Christmas? Or is spring in the air? The only way to answer these ques-tions is to view this property now.
ONLY £76,950

D Comment on the kind of language used in the following. Write a simpler and clearer version.

4.2 It would be wrong to attempt to assess speech as if it were a spoken form of written language. It is necessary to focus upon the extent to which the student is able to achieve a range of communicative purposes, rather than to focus only on features such as grammar or vocabulary. To accommodate a wide range of communicative purposes, the Working Party has sought to include in the criteria situations which involve describing, instructing/directing, informing/expounding, narrating, arguing, persuading, reporting, speculating, advancing hypotheses.

4.3 This wide variety of speech situations demands a correspondingly wide range of language, from informal conversation to formal discussion. There should be an equal emphasis on formal and informal registers, especially as informal registers will be crucial to the further personal and social development of the individual.

Secondary Examinations Council,
ENGLISH – DRAFT GRADE CRITERIA

E Find further examples of each of the different types of stale language outlined in this chapter.

9 ◆ Sentences and Paragraphs

The kinds of sentences and paragraphs writers use can have an effect on the impact of what they write.

Sentences

Sentences can be short or long. The choice will depend on the purpose of the writing and the audience addressed. For instance, short sentences would be appropriate in writing for young children or in instructions or in less demanding tabloid journalism. Short sentences too can help to build up tension and excitement in writing describing actions or feelings.

Longer sentences would be appropriate when addressing a more educated audience, as in quality newspapers or in more serious novels. Longer sentences can help in developing a reasoned argument or in a lengthy, detailed description.

But if all the sentences are short, or if all the sentences are long, there is the danger of monotony. Generally, good writers try to vary the length of their sentences while keeping them appropriate to their purpose and their audience. For instance, a short sentence after a series of long ones can act as a summing up or can make the reader pause for thought. For example:

> The counters and shelves were piled high with a jumble of sweaters and shirts which customers were pulling and picking at and fighting over. The sales assistants had the frantic air of people on the edge of a nervous breakdown as they tried to keep control and wrap up goods and ring the money up in the tills. Everyone was shoving and pushing and grabbing and shouting. It was pandemonium.

Good writers, too, try to vary the type of sentence they use so that they are not all of the same pattern. Different types of sentence are:

The **simple sentence**, consisting of one statement – for example:

> You never walk far through any poor quarter in any big town without coming upon a small newsagent's shop.
>
> *George Orwell,* BOYS' WEEKLIES

The **periodic sentence**, where the thought is developed until the main point is reached at the end – for example:

> Among other public buildings in a certain town, which for many reasons it will be prudent to refrain from mentioning, and to which I will assign no fictitious name, there is one anciently common to most towns, great or small: to wit, a workhouse.
>
> *Charles Dickens,* OLIVER TWIST

The **balanced sentence**, where one idea or statement is balanced or weighed against another – for example:

What we anticipate seldom occurs; what we least expect generally happens.

Benjamin Disraeli, ENDYMION

The **loose sentence**, where phrases or statements are added to each other in a rambling kind of way – for example:

He came to work for me, hating my largesse, lugging his air-compressor up my six flights of stairs, and after a discussion in which his price came down from two hundred to one, and mine rose from fifty dollars to meet his, he left with one of my twenty-dollar bills, the air-compressor on the floor as security, and returned in an hour with so many sacks of whitewash that I had to help him up the stairs.

Norman Mailer, ADVERTISEMENTS FOR MYSELF

Paragraphs

As with sentences, paragraphs can be short or long – a single sentence or a whole page. The choice will depend on the purpose of the writing and the audience addressed. For instance, a series of short paragraphs may help to carry the reader along from point to point. Longer paragraphs may help to develop a point or a description more fully.

Paragraphs should indicate distinct divisions in a piece of writing. Each should be to a certain degree complete in itself. A new thought or a new idea should have a new paragraph. Dividing writing into paragraphs allows the reader to pause for thought between one and the next. Too many short paragraphs may break up the writing too much. Too many long paragraphs may hinder the reader from following the line of thought.

As with sentences, varying the length of paragraphs can be effective. For instance, a short paragraph containing a single sentence after a longer paragraph can alert the reader to an important point or can be dramatic. For example:

He thought of trying to escape, hoping he might be killed in flight rather than by slow torture in the camp, but he never had a chance to try. They were more familiar with escape than he was and, knowing what to expect, they forestalled it. The only other time he had tried to escape from anyone, he had succeeded. When he had left his home in Boston, his father had raged and his grandmother had cried, but they could not talk him out of his intention.

The men of the Crow raiding party didn't bother with talk.

Dorothy M. Johnson, A MAN CALLED HORSE

◆Q◆

A Consider the appropriateness and the effectiveness of the sentences and paragraphs in the following passages.

The monster was only a hundred yards off now, it and the Fog Horn crying at each other. As the lights hit them, the monster's eyes were fire and ice, fire and ice.

"That's life for you," said McDunn. "Someone always waiting for someone who never comes home. Always someone loving some thing more than that thing loves them. And after a while you want to destroy whatever that thing is, so it can't hurt you no more."

The monster was rushing at the lighthouse.

The Fog Horn blew.

"Let's see what happens," said McDunn.

He switched the Fog Horn off.

The ensuing minute of silence was so intense that we could hear our hearts pounding in the glassed area of the tower, could hear the slow greased turn of the light.

The monster stopped and froze. Its great lantern eyes blinked. Its mouth gaped. It gave a sort of rumble, like a volcano. It twitched its head this way and that, as if to seek the sounds now dwindled off into the fog. It peered at the lighthouse. It rumbled again. Then its eyes caught fire. It reared up, threshed the water, and rushed at the tower, its eyes filled with angry torment.

Ray Bradbury, THE FOG HORN

170 hurt at bloody Trafalgar

TWO teenagers were knifed and 170 people injured in one of the most violent New Year celebrations in London's Trafalgar Square.

Fifty-four of the revellers, including both the 17-year-old youths stabbed, were rushed to hospital. All were allowed to go home after treatment.

One hospital official said: "It was a night of sheer madness."

Muggers

There were 139 arrests, most for public disorder and drunkenness, but some people will face robbery charges.

For the first time mounted police were called in to prevent gangs of muggers "steaming" through the 100,000 crowd.

In central London, ambulancemen dealt with a record 834 emergencies in the four hours after midnight.

TODAY

Now you can choose Next from home, with the Next Directory.

Beautiful fashion for men, women and kids – none of it available in the shops.

Stunning shoes, swimwear, sportswear, luggage, accessories and interiors. Lovely lingerie, jewellery and essentials.

Even the book's beautiful.

It's thumb-indexed, with bookmarks. It has real fabric swatches. And there's even a sizing manual and tape measure.

Best of all, you can order by telephone between 8 am and 10 pm 7 days a week and we'll deliver within 48 hours, including evenings and weekends (by the way, wherever you call from it's charged at the local rate).

All in all the whole thing's absolutely unique.

Which brings us to the only drawback. Copies of the Directory are extremely limited So reserve yours by writing or phoning today.

● N O W   Y O U ' R E   T A L K I N G ●

Advertisement for NEXT DIRECTORY

3

4 | Are Your Improvements An Investment?

A few years ago the owners of a period house in the Home Counties found they were in need of some extra space. They decided to 'improve' it with a two-storey extension. An architect was recruited, given carte blanche, and the resulting design was duly implemented.

It was only when the builders reached the first floor level that they realised the design was structurally impossible to carry out . . .

The plans were hastily compromised and the result was a cobbled together effort of two separate extensions, two storeys on the side, one storey on the back. A tiled roof was pitched at 11 degrees – barely enough to let the rain run off – and cost £10,000 to put right. The whole assembly looked totally 'wrong' on a period house, and had an alarming effect on its value.

Rather than the £230,000 the owners could have expected for the property had an appropriate extension been added, they only managed to get £215,000 for it. The work cost £25,000 even with the £10,000 'fix', and though it did increase the size and to some extent the value of the house, the extra value was far less than the money spent. The owners had three years of building and legal problems for little result.

They are not unique in tackling a so-called home 'improvement' which ends up costing them a packet rather than adding value to their principal asset.

Prudential Property Services,
PRESTIGE AND COUNTRY HOMES, HOME COUNTIES SOUTH

10 ◆ Close Reading

When reading a piece of writing, we take in the words immediately in front of us and weigh up their meaning. But we also store up what we have already read and refer back to it in our minds. We think ahead and speculate about how the writing is going to develop. At the end we should be able to have an overall view of the piece of writing.

For instance, consider a piece of writing that presents a point of view. As we read a particular paragraph, we are concerned to understand and interpret what it is saying. But we also hold in our minds what has already been said and think, 'So that is what was meant earlier' or 'But that contradicts what was said at the beginning.' We look ahead and think, 'Now where is this leading us?' or 'I wonder if that piece of evidence will be mentioned.'

It is the same with expressive writing. We may gain an impression of a particular character at the beginning of the novel or story and then have to modify that impression as we learn more about the character. We may think we know how the novel or story is going to end, and then be surprised or have our expectations confirmed.

Reading is not just a passive activity. It is like carrying on a continual dialogue with the writer about the ideas being expressed.

A   Read the following editorial that appeared in the *Evening Standard*. It has been broken up into sections with each section followed by questions designed to encourage you to evaluate what is being said and to look backward and look forward.

Getting away with it

SCHOOLCHILDREN have always been mischievous, and often unruly. They are at an age when getting away with things is an end in itself, and no rational system of education would ever attempt to make them act like responsible adults every minute of the day. But increasingly in recent years we have been witnessing extremes of this behaviour, with children who either resort to a vindictive vandalism, ripping up school property and setting fire to school buildings, or else turn away from the world to drug-taking or hours spent gambling on fruit machines.

- What view does the editorial have of schoolchildren? Do you find it convincing?

- What differences does the editorial claim to find in the behaviour of schoolchildren in recent years? Do you agree?

- What do you think this editorial is going to be about, judging from the title and this opening paragraph?

> Criminal tendencies are easier to deal with, although there isn't much evidence that local education authorities are doing so forcefully enough. According to a Government report published today, Crime Prevention In Schools, the annual cost of vandalism nationally is thought to approach £30 million.
>
> The report criticises local educational authorities for putting too much emphasis (and money) on security equipment in regularly vandalised schools instead of finding head teachers who will improve the school atmosphere and set high standards for pupils and teachers.

- Would you agree that 'criminal tendencies are easier to deal with'?

- What does the editorial suggest would cut down on vandalism? Do you agree with this? What methods might be used?

- What seems to be the purpose of the editorial now?

> This is easier said than done in the minority of run-down, usually inner-city schools where most of the vandalism occurs. But it does at least address the point that child vandalism is often the result of an absence of any kind of authority or moral example provided at home or at school. Where children are not taught the difference between right and wrong, because parents and teachers both think it is the other's business to instil it, then vandalism will increase however many locks, safes or alarms are installed.

- Does the editorial admit that the problem is a difficult one?

- Who does the editorial blame for vandalism and why? Do you find this convincing?

> So will other manifestations of discontent and contempt for authority, such as paint-spraying trains and gambling on fruit-machines. Both are dangerous. An 11-year-old boy was killed recently under a North London Tube train. And the accessibility of fruit machines in chip shops, cafes and amusement arcades is leading to widespread

gambling among teenagers with all the attendant consequences of suicides, truancies, and theft and extortion in the playground to get money to fuel the gambling addiction. Here at least the Government can take direct action. Fruit machines should be banned from places where children can go, and restricted to licensed premises.

– How does this paragraph link up with what has already been said?

– Does 'gambling on fruit machines' show 'contempt for authority'?

– Do you think the editorial paints a fair picture or does it exaggerate?

– What conclusion does the editorial reach? Would this be effective?

– Is this the kind of conclusion you expected from reading the opening paragraph?

– What do you think of the way the argument is presented in the editorial as a whole?

B Read the following story. The author was born in Kingston, Jamaica, and the story is probably set there during the Second World War. Consider each section and the questions that follow in turn.

BLACKOUT

THE city was in partial blackout, the street lights had not been turned on, on account of the wartime policy of conserving electricity, and the houses behind their discreet arelia hedges were wrapped in an atmosphere of exclusive respectability.

The young woman waiting at the bus stop was not in the least nervous, in spite of the wave of panic that had been sweeping the city about bands of hooligans roaming the streets after dark and assaulting unprotected women. She was a sensible young woman to begin with, who realized that one good scream would be sufficient to bring a score of respectable suburban householders running to her assistance. On the other hand she was an American, and fully conscious of the tradition of American young women that they don't scare easily.

Even that slinking blacker shadow that seemed to be slowly materialising out of the darkness at the other side of the street did not disconcert her. She was only slightly curious now that she observed that the shadow was approaching her.

Setting

confident

proud

Interested in world.

Intrusion Language

49

- What factors could give cause for anxiety?
- Why is the young woman not anxious?
- What is her attitude towards the shadow approaching her?
- What suggestions are there in this section as to how the story may develop?

Ex. bo (handwritten)

'slinking' explained (handwritten)

Black (handwritten)

prejudice? (handwritten)

Only notices colour. (handwritten)

Pride amusement (handwritten)

Appearan (handwritten)

'It is his country (handwritten)

?sense of adventure (handwritten)

her problem (handwritten)

he was not an equal (handwritten)

he did not take the ro she expect (handwritten)

It was a young man dressed in conventional shirt and pants, with a pair of canvas shoes on his feet. That was what lent the suggestion of slinking to his movements, because he went along noiselessly; that, and the mere suggestion of a stoop. For he was very tall. And there was a curious look as of a great hunger or unrest about the eyes. But the thing that struck her immediately was the fact that he was black; the other particulars scarcely made any impression at all as against that. In her country it is not every night that a white woman would be likely to be thus nonchalantly approached by a black man. There was enough of novelty in all this to intrigue her. She seemed to remember that any sort of adventure could happen to you in one of these tropical islands of the West Indies.

'Could you give me a light, lady?' the man said. True she was smoking, but she had only just lit this one from the stub of the cigarette she had thrown away. The fact was she had no matches. Would he believe her, she wondered.

'I am sorry, I haven't got a match.'

The young man looked into her face, seemed to hesitate an instant and said, his brow slightly in perplexity: 'But you are smoking.'

There was no argument against that. Still she was not particular about giving him a light from the cigarette she was smoking. It may be stupid, but there was a suggestion of intimacy about such an act, simple as it was, that, call it what you may, she just could not accept offhand.

There was a moment's hesitation on her part now, during which time the man's steady gaze never left her face. There was something of pride and challenge in his look, and curiously mingled with that, something of quiet amusement too.

She held out her cigarette toward him between two fingers.

'Here,' she said, 'you can light from that.'

In the act of bending his head to accept the proffered light, he had perforce to come quite close to her. He did not seem to understand that she meant him to take the lighted cigarette from her hand. He just bent over her hand to light his.

- What feelings does the woman have about the fact that the man is black?
- Is there anything to suggest that the woman is prejudiced?
- What impression do you get of the man and his attitude towards the woman?
- Are the impressions you had of the way the story was going to develop strengthened or altered by what happens in this section?

Ex book

Suggestion of poverty

why? Prejudice?

Waste?

Contempt

Presently he straightened up, inhaled a deep lungful of soothing smoke and exhaled again with satisfaction. She saw then that he was smoking the half of a cigarette, that had been clinched and saved for future consumption.

'Thank you,' said the man, politely; and was in the act of moving off when he noticed that instead of returning her cigarette to her lips she had casually, unthinkingly flicked it away. He observed all these things in the split part of a second that it took him to say those two words. It was almost a whole cigarette she had thrown away. She had been smoking it with evident enjoyment a moment before.

He stood there looking at her, with a sort of cold speculation.

In a way it unnerved her. Not that she was frightened. He seemed quite decent in his own way, and harmless; but he made her feel uncomfortable. If he had said something rude she would have preferred it. It would have been no more than she would have expected of him. But instead, this quiet contemptuous look. Yes, that was it. The thing began to take on definition in her mind. How dare he; the insolence!

'Well, what are you waiting for?' she said, because she felt she had to break the tension somehow.

'I am sorry I made you waste a whole cigarette,' he said.

She laughed a little nervously. 'It's nothing,' she said, feeling a fool.

'There's plenty more where that came from, eh?'

'I suppose so.'

This would not do. She had no intention of standing at a street corner jawing with – well, with a black man. There was something indecent about it. Why didn't he move on? As though he had read her thoughts he said:

'This is the street lady. It's public.'

Well, anyway she didn't have to answer him. She could snub him quietly, the way she should have properly done from the start.

'It's a good thing you're a woman,' he said.

'And if I were a man?'

Prejudice

'As man to man maybe I'd give you something to think about,' he said, still in that quiet even voice.
— In America they lynched them for less than that, she thought.
'This isn't America,' he said. 'I can see you are an American. In this country there are only men and women. You'll learn about that if you stop here long enough.'
This was too much. But there was nothing she could do about it. But yes there was. She could humour him. Find out what his ideas were about this question, anyway. It would be something to talk about back home. Suddenly she was intrigued.

them

never a human being

he become a novelt...

– What is the significance of the fact that the man is smoking half a cigarette?

– Why does the woman throw away almost a whole cigarette? What is the man's attitude to this?

– Consider the different feelings the woman has about the man. Have these feelings already been indicated in the previous section?

– Why do you think the woman is 'intrigued'?

'So in this country there are only men and women, eh?'
'That's right. So to speak there is only you an' me, only there are hundreds of thousands of us. We seem to get along somehow without lynchings and burnings and all that.'
'Do you really think that all men are created equal?'
'It don't seem to me there is any sense in that. The facts show it ain't so. Look at you an' me, for instance. But that isn't to say you're not a woman the same way as I am a man. You see what I mean?'
'I can't say I do.'
'You will though, if you stop here long enough.'
She threw a quick glance in his direction.
The man laughed.
'I don't mean what you're thinking,' he said. 'You're not my type of woman. You don't have anything to fear under that heading.'
'Oh!'
'You're waiting for the bus, I take it. Well that's it coming now. Thanks for the light.'
'Don't mention it,' she said, with a nervous sort of giggle.

Jamaica

She misunderstands

disappointed?

insulted?

– What comparison does the man make between Jamaica and the USA at the time?

– Describe his views on equality and men and women.

– What incident has already illustrated that people are not equal?

– Do you think the woman would find the man's comment 'You're not my type of woman' reassuring or disappointing?

Oh!

> He made no attempt to move along as the bus came up. He stood there quietly aloof, as though in the consciousness of a male strength and pride that was just his. There was something about him that was at once challenging and disturbing. He had shaken her supreme confidence in some important sense.
>
> As the bus moved off she was conscious of his eyes' quiet scrutiny of her, without the interruption of artificial barriers; in the sense of dispassionate appraisement, as between man and woman; any man, any woman.
>
> She fought resolutely against the very natural desire to turn her head and take a last look at him. Perhaps she was thinking about what the people on the bus might think. And perhaps it was just as well that she did not see him bend forward with that swift hungry movement, retrieving from the gutter the half-smoked cigarette she had thrown away.
>
> *Roger Mais*

he has gained the upper ground

she felt superior white-American

he has rejected her as a woman she is not his type.

– In what way has the woman been disturbed by the encounter?

– Why does the woman want to take a last look at the man?

– What is ironic about the last sentence?

– Does this last sentence reinforce what you have learned about the man or does it show him in a new light?

– Looking back at the story as a whole, what points do you think the author was trying to make?

11 ◆ Structure and Development

The structure or shape of a piece of writing and the way it is developed can affect its success or otherwise. Most writers organise and reorganise what they write until they find the most effective form.

Probably the simplest kind of structure is for a piece of writing to have a beginning, a middle and an end (or an introduction, a development and a conclusion). But there are other kinds of structure. Here are some examples:

- A story might begin at the end, with the events then being seen as a kind of flashback

- A story might begin at a dramatic point in the middle, go back to explain how this point was reached, and then continue by saying what happens next

- A story might begin with a description of the main character or setting and then say what happened to that character or what happened in that setting

- An essay or an article might begin with an example or an anecdote and then go on to the basic point the writer is making

- A story or an essay might be built out of the contrast between two characters or two points of view

- A novel or a play might be constructed in such a way that all its characters and incidents cast light on a central theme such as bravery or greed

- An essay or an article might be built up of a series of questions

- A poem might consist of a description and a contrast or an account of an incident and a concluding thought

- An essay or an article might be constructed out of a comparison of the past with the present or the attitudes of the young with the attitudes of the old.

In order to identify the structure of a piece of writing, you have to be able to break the writing down into its various sections or stages and see how these are related to each other. You have to get an overall impression of the piece of writing so that you can see how the different parts fit together.

It is possible that a particular subject could be treated in a number of different ways. But good writers seek the best way (the best form and structure) to express what they have to say. If the form and structure chosen are effective, they should help to reinforce what the writer is saying and give it greater impact.

A Examine the following examples. Describe the structure and development of each and comment on the contribution that its structure and development make to the effectiveness of what is being said.

1

A GIRL named Christine took me behind the bikeshed at Hinckley Grammar School 25 years ago this month and showed me something that changed my life. It was the first single by a group from Liverpool called the Beatles.

Being 14 in 1962 was wonderful. Being 39 in 1987 isn't. One thing that keeps me going as I lurch towards my 40th birthday is the memories of the Sixties. You see, the Beatles really did change my life.

Love Me Do, the first single from the fab four crept rather than rocketed into the charts 25 years ago this week. The mega hits came later but the mournful harmonica riff cut through the dross on the radio at the time like so much corrosive acid.

You should have been there. From the first moment I heard the Beatles I knew what I was going to do. No more studying for O levels. I was going to be a pop star.

Being an eminently sensible

14-year-old I had a backup plan. If I wasn't good enough to be a musician I'd be a music critic.

It was almost that simple. If it hadn't been for John, Paul, George and Ringo I'd have worked hard at school and become a brain surgeon. Instead, like most frustrated musicians, I became a music critic.

The music speaks for itself still. The impact of their personalities throughout the whole world was something else.

To put things into perspective, pick any successful group out of this week's chart and imagine anybody over 20 knowing all of their Christian names.

Then try to imagine Prince Philip sending them a telegram, The Sunday Times' music critic calling them "the greatest composers since Beethoven" or The Times Educational Supplement pointing out that their lyrics

"represent an important barometer in our society."

And if you think your favourite group, sorry band, sells a lot of records try and imagine its next single having three million advance orders. (Can't Buy Me Love). In 1964 the Beatles occupied all top five positions in US charts with combined sales exceeding 13 million.

In 1967 one million fans in America ordered Sgt Pepper without hearing a track. In 1970 the Let It Be album achieved the highest initial sale in the history of recorded music – 3¾ million advance orders, almost $26 million.

They conquered the world, revolutionised popular music and sold an awful lot of records. And it all began in October, 25 years ago.

Thanks for the memory. Thanks John, Paul, George and Ringo. Thanks Christine.

Martyn Sutton,
JUNIOR GUARDIAN

2

Let me not to the marriage of true minds
Admit impediments. Love is not love
Which alters when it alteration finds,
Or bends with the remover to remove:
O, no! it is an ever-fixèd mark,
That looks on tempests and is never shaken;
It is the star to every wandering bark,
Whose worth's unknown, although his height be taken.
Love's not Time's fool, though rosy lips and cheeks
Within his bending sickle's compass come;
Love alters not with his brief hours and weeks,
But bears it out even to the edge of doom.
    If this be error, and upon me proved,
    I never writ, nor no man ever loved.

William Shakespeare

3

Accident

A WOMAN was sitting in a café about eleven o'clock one morning, taking sips from a cup of weak tea and eating a cream bun, without knowing she was doing so. She had a bad headache.

On the chair by her side – there were four chairs altogether around the table – she had placed a pair of thin brown gloves and a handbag. She kept looking at these from time to time. They were smeared with drying blood, as was the front of her dress; and each time she looked at them she groaned audibly.

Two waitresses, not yet in their uniforms, still occupied with cleaning out the café, ready for the lunch-hour rush, kept peering at her from the door of the kitchen. Every now and then the cook joined them, and they all cast puzzled glances at their solitary customer, eating and drinking like an automaton.

The name of this woman was Mrs Leveritt. She was between forty and forty-five years of age, and had brown eyes and a clear skin. Normally, she would have colour, but just now her face was drawn and pale. She did not seem to notice the waitresses or the cook, but was utterly possessed with one inward thought, to the exclusion of anything else.

She had a husband and three children. Not having married until she was almost thirty, her children were still quite young – indeed, they were all at school. Her husband was a joiner. She had married him because he had come after her for several years, and she liked him.

When she was young, she had been full of romance, a very high-handed girl. She wasn't going to marry anybody just for the sake of getting married. She was going to wait until somebody came with whom she could fall in love. She knew exactly how it would happen; she would see him, know him in a moment. This would be the man for whom she would leave father, mother, and home. There would be no mistake; they would both know.

But first her mother died, then her father. Fred Leveritt, who came to the house every Wednesday and Saturday — pretending to come for her father's sake, but really, she knew, to see her — had told her that the best thing she could do was to marry him. She was very fond of Fred, he was most kind, and he thought the world about her. So she had married Fred.

How calm and happy her life had been with him. She looked no older than when she was married. Her three children had suffered only from minor ailments, except Phyllis, the eldest, who had once had to go to hospital with fever. Their home was comfortable. Fred had made a great deal of the furniture, and she kept it polished bright and shining. Every year, for one week, they went to the seaside with the children, and had a good time, whether the weather was wet or fine.

This morning she had set off, soon after getting the children to school, to do some ordinary shopping. She wanted to make a steak and kidney pie for dinner. Just as she got to the cross-roads she saw there was an accident.

She had been looking into a shop window as she walked on and did not actually see the accident happen. But there was a lorry, and a boy with a sick white face climbing out of the driver's seat; and, on the ground, some yards away, a man was lying.

Mrs Leveritt's first impulse was to run away. Indeed, her feet actually turned, and when she came to her normal, kindly senses, she was going rather rapidly in another direction. With just such another whirl, she turned; and she was the one on whose knee the injured man's head was pillowed, and hers was the face on which he looked as he opened his eyes.

What happened next, Mrs Leveritt was not sure. There must have been a crowd of people, and the boy coming limping up out of the lorry, and a policeman somewhere. There must have been somebody ringing up in the nearby telephone-box for an ambulance, because soon one came.

But for Mrs Leveritt, and the man whose head she held in her arms, there was a moment of complete understanding. It was as if the world had stopped around them, and they were enclosed in a lovely crystal ball, looking for ever into each other's eyes, made perfect by love.

The crystal ball burst with a crash. Before she could draw her thoughts again into focus, everything had disappeared; the man, the ambulance, the policeman, the crowd. She had not seen the accident happen, therefore she was of no use as a witness. She walked a long way before, at last, she entered the café and ordered tea. The waitress put some stale cakes near her, and she ate mechanically.

At last she had to go home. Realizing that there was no time to make the pie, she hastily prepared a plainer dinner for the children, looked after their needs, and sent them off to school again.

In the evening, after her husband had come home and had his

meal, a knock came at the door. She was washing up. Hastily drying her hands on her apron she ran to open the door. She was expecting a message. She knew not what, nor when it would come, but that it would reach her she was certain.

However, it was only Ted Rhodes, a friend of Fred's. Ted was also a joiner, but he was mostly on outside work, and was often a little stiff with rheumatism. The two men smoked and talked, and, for some reason, as soon as her work was done, the woman sat and listened to every word attentively. At the same time the other half of her brain was wondering when she could go to the hospital to visit the injured man, and if they would let her see him.

Suddenly Ted said, 'A mate o' mine was run over with a lorry this morning and killed. Kitson, 'is name was. Lived over other side o' Shawford, near brickworks.'

Fred didn't know him.

Mrs Leveritt gave a great sigh. Here was the message.

'What was he like?' she asked, twisting her lips into a solemn smile.

'Like? Let me see,' said Ted. He thought for a minute. 'A tall chap, wi' greyish 'air and plenty o' colour. D'you know 'im?'

'I think so,' she answered, very quietly.

A tall chap, with greyish hair and plenty of colour. That was all she had to remember. And he had gone out into the dark, taking her love with him.

Malachi Whitaker

B Examine the structure and development of a novel or play you have read recently. Comment on the contribution structure and development make to the effectiveness of the novel or play.

12 ◆ Different Styles

Not all writers employ the same style in their writing all the time. The way writers write will vary according to a number of factors – the purpose of the writing, the kind of writing it is and the subject matter, the audience it is intended for.

But often, for some individual writers, these factors remain more or less constant whatever they are writing. Some novelists, for instance, write with the same purpose, the same kind of subject matter for the same kind of audience in all their novels. They develop an individual style of their own – a style that can be recognised and distinguished from the way that other novelists write. The writing of Jane Austen, for instance, is very different from the writing of Charles Dickens.

The same is true of particular newspaper columnists and newspapers in general. The way a tabloid newspaper is written is normally very different from the way a quality newspaper is written.

In order to identify the particular features of the style of a piece of writing, you should look at:

– the language used
– the use of figurative language
– the sentence structure
– the paragraphing
– the tone
– how appropriate the style is to the purpose of the writing, the subject matter and the audience intended.

A Examine the passages on the next three pages. Identify and illustrate the significant features of each, and comment on their appropriateness and effectiveness. It may be a help to follow the approach used in Chapter 10.

① MIRROR COMMENT

Burning issue

THERE are killer sofas and chairs in millions of homes. But not in Anne and John Burke's any longer.

For the safety of their three children they are doing away with their three-piece suite because it contains dangerous polyurethane foam.

If everyone did the same, we could all end up sitting on the floor.

Furniture stores are crammed with suites which are just as dangerous. A spot check shows that some sales staff don't know that, some don't care and some even remove the warning red triangles.

There's only one word for that conduct: CRIMINAL.

Furniture makers are behaving much worse. They are trying to con the Government into letting them continue to turn out death traps.

Liars

Tests by the Daily Mirror have proved that the high-resilience foam they are promoting is no safer than standard foam.

There's only one word to describe them: LIARS.

Yesterday Habitat said it will encourage customers to buy suites made with fire-retardant foam. But it will go on selling the others.

In the end, the only way to guarantee that new sofas are safe is for the Government to ban all fillings that aren't fire-retardant.

There'll be only one word to describe Ministers if they don't rush that through Parliament: FOOLS.

DAILY MIRROR

②

WHOSOEVER has observed that sedate and clerical bird, the rook, may perhaps have noticed that when he wings his way homeward towards nightfall, in a sedate and clerical company, two rooks will suddenly detach themselves from the rest, will retrace their flight for some distance, and will there poise and linger; conveying to mere men the fancy that it is of some occult importance to the body politic, that this artful couple should pretend to have renounced connection with it.

Similarly, service being over in the old Cathedral with the square tower, and the choir scuffling out again, and divers venerable persons of rook-like aspect dispersing, two of these latter retrace their steps, and walk together in the echoing Close.

Not only is the day waning, but the year. The low sun is fiery and yet cold behind the monastery ruin, and the Virginia creeper on the Cathedral wall has showered half its deep-red leaves down on the pavement. There has been rain this afternoon, and a wintry shudder goes among the little pools on the cracked, uneven flagstones, and through the giant elm-trees as they shed a gust of tears. Their fallen leaves lie strewn thickly about. Some of these leaves, in a timid rush, seek sanctuary within the low arched Cathedral door; but two men coming out resist them, and cast them forth again with their feet; this done, one of the two locks the door with a goodly key, and the other flits away with a folio music-book.

Charles Dickens, THE MYSTERY OF EDWIN DROOD

3

EVERY neighbourhood should have a great lady. The great lady of Sanditon was Lady Denham; and in their journey from Willingden to the coast, Mr Parker gave Charlotte a more detailed account of her than had been called for before. She had been necessarily often mentioned at Willingden – for being his colleague in speculation, Sanditon itself could not be talked of long without the introduction of Lady Denham. That she was a very rich old lady, who had buried two husbands, who knew the value of money, and was very much looked up to and had a poor cousin living with her, were facts already known; but some further particulars of her history and her character served to lighten the tediousness of a long hill, or a heavy bit of road, and to give the visiting young lady a suitable knowledge of the person with whom she might now expect to be daily associating.

Lady Denham had been a rich Miss Brereton, born to wealth but not to education. Her first husband had been a Mr Hollis, a man of considerable property in the country, of which a large share of the parish of Sanditon, with manor and mansion house, made a part. He had been an elderly man when she married him, her own age about thirty. Her motives for such a match could be little understood at the distance of forty years, but she had so well nursed and pleased Mr Hollis that at his death he left her everything – all his estates, and all at her disposal.

Jane Austen, SANDITON

4

Our just deserts

FORESTS, it is said, precede mankind. Deserts follow. It seems to be no accident that the fallen columns and broken statues of past civilisations often lie on devastated ground. The ruined cities of North Africa, once flowing with wheat and olive oil, now stagnant in the sand; the bare hills of Attica, mourned by Plato as 'skeletons' of what they had been; the Maowusu desert of Inner Mongolia that overtook the lush pasture-land, alive with deer that Genghis Khan chose for his tomb: all testify to the truth that when the land is overexploited, everything else collapses.

No civilisation, however, has set about consuming its future with such enthusiasm as our own. And none before us has done it on a global, rather than local scale. In the last ten years productive land the size of the 12 countries of the EEC has been turned to dust. And the United Nations Environment Programme warns that one third of the entire land surface of the world is now in danger. 850 million people, more than one in every six alive, are already suffering from this man-made disaster. By the year 2000, little more than a decade away, 1,200 million will be hit. The recurring famine now threatening Ethiopia and the worst drought in a century increasing its grip on India are not merely linked to this process. They are also harbingers of far worse to come.

Ten years ago this weekend a special UN Conference opened at which the world solemnly agreed a package of measures to halt the spread of the deserts by the year 2000. Since then virtually nothing has been done. Rich countries have failed to provide the money they promised; poor countries have failed to show any interest, even when their own croplands disappeared into the sand. The hundreds of millions of people most affected, always among the poorest and most disorganised, have been powerless to make their Governments fulfil their undertakings.

The causes of this massive loss of ground remain, as the world agreed ten years ago, over-cultivation, overgrazing, and the cutting down of trees. The solutions then resolved upon remain technically practicable, and far cheaper than the cost of losing the land. The urgency is now infinitely greater. The world must act upon what it formally adopted ten years ago — and fast — before the very foundations of our civilisation crumble in the sand.

THE OBSERVER

B Find two passages which are written in very different styles. Explain the differences between them.

Part Two

Looking at Particular
Aspects of Language

13◆Facts and Figures

Disraeli said, 'There are lies, damned lies and statistics.' What do you think he meant?

Statistics are sets of figures produced usually as the result of a survey or research. In themselves, statistics mean very little. What gives them meaning is the comparison of one set of statistics with another and the way these figures are then interpreted. The same set of statistics can mean different things to different people. They can be misused and manipulated. People can select from them what they want.

For instance, a firm's sales figures may be something like this:

Jan	100
Feb	96
Mar	87
Apr	75
May	73
Jun	62
Jul	59
Aug	49
Sep	45
Oct	36
Nov	51
Dec	72

The sales manager may boast that sales increased by 100 per cent over the last three months. That would be true, but it gives a very misleading impression of the movement of sales throughout the year.

Often statistics are expressed in the form of a graph or a diagram. These can be useful because they cram a lot of information into a small space, they organise the information into a form which makes it easier to make comparisons and draw conclusions, and they can also present the information in a way that gives it greater impact.

When interpreting material of this kind, you have to examine it carefully and make sure you understand what the blocks or columns represent before you can compare one with another. With a graph, you need to grasp the significance of the horizontal and vertical scales before you can work out what the graph is about. Study the diagram or graph slowly detail by detail. Make sure you understand clearly what the statistics or the figures represent. Ask yourself which figures are higher and which are lower and what that means.

A Look at the way information is presented in the diagram and article over the page.

THEM AND US—PAY INCREASES FOR MAJOR SECTIONS OF THE WORKFORCE 1985/6

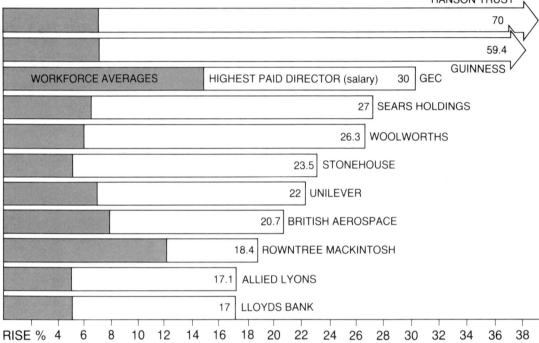

ERNEST
SAUNDERS
(GUINNESS)
£330,000

LORD
HANSON
(HANSON TRUST)
£301,000

LORD
WEINSTOCK
(GEC)
£177,200

MAITLAND-
SMITH
(SEARS)
£153,795

SIR DERRICK
HOLDEN-BROWN
(ALLIED LYONS)
£146,238

JOHN
BECKETT*
(WOOLWORTHS)
£144,000

SIR AUSTIN
PEARCE
(AEROSPACE)
£121,660

KENNETH
DIXON
(ROWNTREE)
£103,000

HANSON TRUST — 70

GUINNESS — 59.4

WORKFORCE AVERAGES · HIGHEST PAID DIRECTOR (salary) 30 GEC

27 SEARS HOLDINGS

26.3 WOOLWORTHS

23.5 STONEHOUSE

22 UNILEVER

20.7 BRITISH AEROSPACE

18.4 ROWNTREE MACKINTOSH

17.1 ALLIED LYONS

17 LLOYDS BANK

RISE % 4 6 8 10 12 14 16 18 20 22 24 26 28 30 32 34 36 38

SOURCE—BARGAINING REPORTS, 1 SEPT *NO LONGER CHAIRMAN

HOW BOSSES STRIKE IT RICH

THE SPECTACULAR 59 per cent pay rise awarded to Mr Ernest Saunders, chief executive of Guinness, highlights the disparity between increases given to leaders of Britain's biggest companies and those received by their employees, *writes Steve Vines.*

A survey to be published next week confirms that the pay award to Mr Saunders, totalling £175,000, is far from an isolated case.

Ministers will be less than pleased to see that one of their biggest backers, Lord Hanson, chairman of Hanson Trust, tops the league with a 70 per cent rise, while the average level of workforce increases in Hanson companies like Imperial Tobacco and Courage Breweries is between 6 and 7.5 per cent.

The comparisons are from the Labour Research Department's 'Bargaining Report', which con-

trasts increases for directors and workers in 22 companies. It found that the average rise for all directors was 18.4 per cent and for other employees just below 7 per cent.

The survey mentions one company that has reduced directors' pay after poor profit performance. Mr Sam Toy, Ford's managing director, took a cut of 19 per cent, leaving his salary at £127,286.

THE OBSERVER

1 Sum up the points being made by the diagram and the article opposite.

2 Comment on the visual impact of the diagram.

3 What information is given in the article that is not represented in the diagram?

4 Do you think the diagram or the article show bias of any kind or do they make fair comment?

B Study the two graphs below. Write a paragraph (about ten lines) on unemployment in the UK in the 1930s and 1980s compared with international unemployment. Use only information given here.

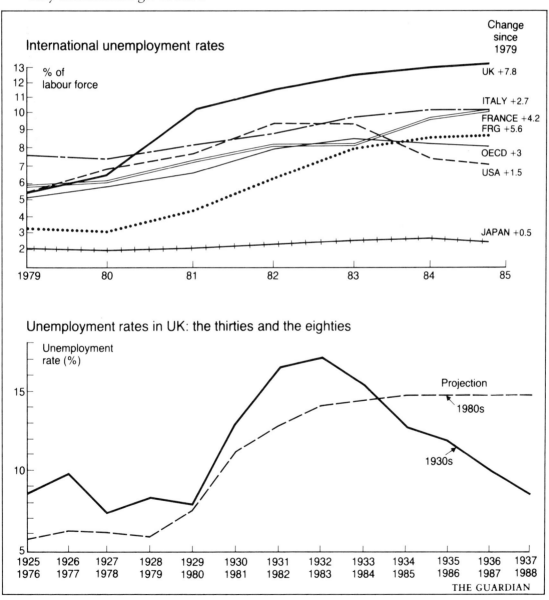

C Read the following account of a consultative paper on equality of opportunity in employment in Northern Ireland.

Catholics still lose out in job market

The gap in academic attainment between Protestant and Catholic school-leavers in Northern Ireland has progressively narrowed, with little difference in results when schools of the same type are compared.

The trend among Protestants to opt overwhelmingly for grammar schools is helping perpetuate the pattern where they record better O and A level exam results than Catholics – thus gaining an advantage in the job market.

A consultative paper on equality of opportunity in employment, launched by Mr Tom King, Northern Ireland Secretary of State, shows that when the 1984 grammar school intake was surveyed, fee-payers accounted for only 3 per cent in Catholic grammar schools but 8 per cent in the Protestant sector.

Protestants also feature more in the review system for entry to grammar schools after the age of 11. Twice as many Catholics as Protestants opt not to take up grammar school places.

While the number of Catholics entering grammar schools is consistent with their proportion in the transfer age group, the document considers the movement between secondary and grammar schools in the Protestant sector "significantly disproportionate".

It adds: "Within the grammar and secondary sectors separately Catholic pupils attain similar levels of academic achievement as Protestant pupils. However, overall, Catholic pupils fell behind Protestant pupils relatively due to the imbalance between the numbers of Catholics and Protestants attending grammar schools."

This differential is reflected in the qualifications each group of school-leavers brings to the labour market. In 1984 almost 20 per cent of Protestant school-leavers had two or more A levels, compared with just under 17 per cent of Catholics. While 18 per cent of Protestants left school without any GCE/CSE qualifications, the figure for Catholics was almost 25 per cent.

Differences in subject choices were also discerned. Protestants opted for maths and science, while Catholics, particularly those in girls' schools, chose arts and humanities. In 1984 A level science was studied by 31 per cent of Protestant pupils, compared with 23 per cent of Catholic. On the other hand, 46 per cent of Catholic pupils studied arts A levels compared with 37 per cent of Protestants.

The document, which has been circulated as a preliminary to a Charter for Employment Equity, states that Catholic and Protestant school-leavers experience different degrees of success in the job market. While those with no qualifications are equally disadvantaged, Catholics with the same level of academic attainment as Protestants do not enjoy similar advantages.

"Though some educational differences remain, there has been a progressive convergence in academic attainment at point of entry to the labour market. Despite this, there has been relatively little change in the Catholic share of that market either in quantitative or qualitative terms."

Carmel McQuaid, THE TIMES EDUCATIONAL SUPPLEMENT

1   In table form, summarise the statistics given about the differences between Catholics and Protestants in education and employment.

2   What conclusions does the consultative paper come to regarding equality of opportunity (or lack of it) between Catholics and Protestants in education and employment? Do you think these conclusions are justified by the statistics given?

3   Comment on the effectiveness or otherwise of the style in which the consultative paper is written judging from the quotations given here.

4   As far as you can tell, do you think the article presents a fair impression of the content and findings of the consultative paper?

14◆Directions, Explanations and Instructions

In many aspects of life, in undertaking many activities, it is essential to be able to understand directions, explanations and instructions. These can range from baking a cake to repairing a puncture, from filling in a form to growing geraniums.

Usually, if writing of this kind is effective, it is written in simple language and in short direct sentences. To understand and follow it, you need to:

– read it carefully

– examine each point separately, step by step, and make sure you understand what it means

– study any diagrams or illustrations there may be and relate them to the written text.

A Find an example of a piece of writing that gives directions, an explanation or instructions (for example, car manuals, recipe books, information leaflets). Explain why you consider it to be a good or a bad example.

B Compare the two accounts opposite of how to deal with a gas leak.

   1 Which do you think is more effective and why?

   2 Imagine you smell gas in the kitchen when you get up one morning. Write an account of what you do, using information given here.

1

HOW TO HANDLE GAS

1 DON'T strike a match if you smell gas and DO open all windows immediately. Also extinguish fires, naked flames and cigarettes. Make sure that a gas tap has not been left on accidentally or a pilot light blown out. Turn off the supply at the meter control tap and even if you are in doubt telephone Gas Service immediately (look under 'gas' in the telephone directory).

2 Never look for a gas leak with a naked flame. Remember British Gas specialists are the experts when it comes to gas. If there is a leak in the service pipe supplying the meter or in the meter itself, generally no charge is made for repairs. Don't turn the gas on again until the gasman tells you it's safe to do so.

Shirley Conran, SUPERWOMAN

2

DO'S AND DON'TS THAT COULD HELP YOU SURVIVE A GAS LEAK

DO'S

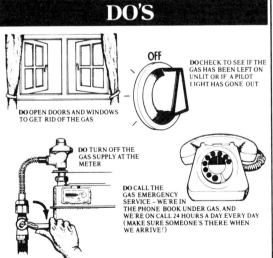

DO OPEN DOORS AND WINDOWS TO GET RID OF THE GAS

DO CHECK TO SEE IF THE GAS HAS BEEN LEFT ON UNLIT OR IF A PILOT LIGHT HAS GONE OUT

DO TURN OFF THE GAS SUPPLY AT THE METER

DO CALL THE GAS EMERGENCY SERVICE – WE'RE IN THE PHONE BOOK UNDER GAS, AND WE'RE ON CALL 24 HOURS A DAY EVERY DAY (MAKE SURE SOMEONE'S THERE WHEN WE ARRIVE!)

DON'TS

DON'T OPERATE ELECTRICAL SWITCHES – ON OR OFF

DON'T SMOKE

DON'T USE NAKED FLAMES

DON'T LEAVE IT TO SOMEONE ELSE – CALL THE EMERGENCY SERVICE.

British Gas
CARING FOR YOUR SAFETY

USE THIS SPACE TO NOTE DOWN YOUR GAS EMERGENCY SERVICE PHONE NUMBER – LOOK IT UP NOW!

CUT THIS ADVERTISEMENT OUT AND KEEP IT SOMEWHERE HANDY. IT COULD SAVE YOUR LIFE.

Advertisement for BRITISH GAS

C How effective do you think this explanation of the dangers of lead in paintwork is? Try to reduce it to a simpler account using short direct sentences.

Department of the Environment
and Welsh Office
INFORMATION NOTE
ON
LEAD IN PAINTWORK

Lead in old paint can be a health hazard. It is the commonest cause of lead poisoning in children, and it can seriously affect even adults.
If you are a parent or adviser to parents or do-it-yourselfers, or in charge of children or their homes or schools, then read this note about the risks and how to avoid them.

Why worry about leaded paintwork?
Undisturbed, leaded paintwork does no harm. But in high concentrations lead and its compounds are poisonous to human beings, and may, if recent research findings are confirmed, have harmful effects even at moderate concentrations – especially on young children. If a child repeatedly eats small fragments of highly leaded paintwork, it can suffer overt poisoning, even death. Fortunately, this is now an extremely rare event in Britain. But it is possible to take in amounts of lead too large to be safe even for an adult through breathing in air contaminated by dust from rubbing down leaded paintwork – or through eating food contaminated by such leaded dust or pieces of crumbling leaded paintwork. In these circumstances, the lead in the paintwork is released to the human environment and becomes a hazard to health.

Why is there lead in paintwork?
Lead – in practice, its compounds – has three possible roles in paint: to make certain colours; to make a weather-resistant coating; and to make it dry more rapidly. (At the extreme, some Victorian domestic paintwork has been found with over 40% lead in it.) In recent years, however, technical developments have produced good substitutes for both the colour and coating functions, with the limited exception of corrosion-resistant primers for steelwork in exposed positions. As a result, most of the lead in paint on retail sale in Britain today is there in the form of driers, and it usually amounts to less than 1% by weight of the dried film. Some paints, however, including specialised metal primers and some white-lead wood primers, have much higher lead contents; and although such paints are normally for trade or industrial use, some are available to non-specialists who may misuse them.

Where is leaded paintwork found?
It requires expensive chemical analysis before one can say with any certainty whether or not a particular piece of paintwork has a significant lead content. But history gives a useful general guide. Before the First World War, lead-based paint was used very extensively on walls, wood and metal, both indoors and outdoors. All paintwork and priming thought to date from before the First World War is likely to contain significant amounts of lead. Technical changes after about 1920 caused steady reductions in both the average lead content of leaded paints and their use, first for indoor work, and later even for outdoor priming. So leaded paintwork is very likely to be found on the exteriors of inter-war buildings and is not uncommon on interior surfaces, especially in the priming coats. It is far less common in the vast majority of domestic premises built since

1945, although there is always the chance that unsuitable leaded paint or primer may have been used. It must also be borne in mind that: (a) recent unleaded paintwork may conceal older, lead-based paint or primer; and (b) older woodwork may have some leaded primer left on it after it has been stripped. Exterior metalwork of whatever age is very likely to have at least a lead-based primer on it unless it has been stripped recently and deliberately repainted with low-lead paint and primer.

Are all pre-Second War buildings dangerous?

Leaded paintwork only becomes a serious hazard when it is disturbed, and then only if the disturbance is such that people breathe or eat dust or debris. Sound paintwork, free from peeling, cracking, chipping or other deterioration, poses no problem. Although leaded paintwork can probably be found in some millions of homes, schools and other similar buildings, the people – whether adults or children – who use them are safe as long as the paintwork is looked after properly.

Children and leaded paintwork

There is, however, a special risk for certain young children. Infants, especially when teething, commonly mouth solid objects or put things they find on the floor into their mouths and chew them: in the worst case this can amount to a medical disorder called 'pica' – an abnormal craving to eat non-food materials. If a child chews sound paintwork or picks up and eats fragments of damaged paintwork from the floor, the chances of consuming a dangerous amount of lead are increased. And, since some lead compounds used in paint are sweet, a child can develop a liking for leaded paint! The risk for a small child from sound paintwork is, of course, mainly from accessible places, within a few feet of the floor: windowsills and door edges are particularly likely to be chewed.

What can be done with suspect paintwork?

In general, and where pica is not a problem, paintwork should be checked to see that it is sound, and that no dust or debris sanded or chipped off it is lurking in corners, crevices or carpets. If paintwork is satisfactory, it should, if possible, be left undisturbed. It is sufficient to paint over it in the normal course of redecorating – or to apply some other form of proprietary surface covering – which may well help to prevent subsequent deterioration or damage to it.

Where a child has pica, the only completely reliable safety measure is to remove the child to a place which is known to be free from leaded paint, especially on accessible surfaces. Failing that, the child should be closely supervised and all accessible surfaces in the home should be stripped with care and repainted with low-lead paint.

When special measures are needed to protect a child, when leaded paintwork is deteriorating, or when structural alterations to a building are needed, it is clearly not possible to leave the paintwork undisturbed. Inevitably, some of it, at least, must be stripped – although it is best to keep this to a minimum as the process of stripping itself releases the lead to the environment, increasing the possible hazard.

Department of the Environment and Welsh Office

15◆Characters

How do fiction writers make their characters 'come alive' from the printed page? Often when we read fiction, we feel we know the people we are reading about. We can visualise them. We know why they behave the way they do and how they will react in other situations.

To enable us to do this, writers may select from a range of devices. They may:

− describe physical appearance

− tell us directly what characters are like

− give details of the characters' background or previous life

− allow characters to reveal themselves through their own words and thoughts

− tell us what other characters think and say about them

− show them reacting to a situation or a moral dilemma in a way that is typical of them

− use language to colour the impression given of the characters.

A Study the passages on the next two pages. Say what you learn about the characters depicted and describe the methods the writers use to give an insight into the characters and their attitudes.

I'm sixteen. I left school last July. No tears, you can bet; I'd been aching to get out since I was fourteen. Couldn't seem to learn any more. Well, I haven't got my dad's head. None of us has, saving Vlady. Talking of favourites, he's my favourite brother. But I'm not his favourite sister. He thinks I'm stupid. Though he used to help me a bit with my schoolwork when he had the patience. Maths and that I never could do, never got the hang of it somehow. English was my best subject. I've got this good imagination, I could always invent stuff. Trouble was my spelling.

Once I wrote this smashing story about a girl who gets mixed up with a black boy (I fancied one myself a bit at the time). I just wrote and wrote. I wrote half the night, and my writing got ropier and my spelling got weirder, but I was carried away. I couldn't be bothered to copy all that out again of course, so next day I handed it in. Miss Nelson, my teacher, always gave me good marks before, but this time do you know what she wrote on the bottom? *One out of ten.* "One for effort," she said but the spelling ruined it.

I never tried for her after that. I used to write bits at home sometimes, but I never did another good thing for her. Cow.

Lynne Reid Banks, THE WRITING ON THE WALL

We'd come, now, through the worst part of the commando course that a visit to my father resembled. It was the moment – that arrived on each of these occasions – when, with everyone stinging and sore, I realised he was glad we were there.

It was never anything but a nervous strain to be with him. Kate at times would turn actually white. He could leave no statement of anyone's unshaken – would take any small remark and hang it on the line like a carpet and beat it remorselessly. No avenue was too trivial for him to explore. He couldn't bear you to have anything to say for what you had or preferred, if it was not what he had or preferred. His refusal of the ordinary give and take of discussion, and his perpetual suspicion that a simple remark concealed some more elaborate one, were deeply exhausting. He looked under every statement for its real meaning, never able to accept that people might speak in, as it were, the clear. 'Hmm!' he would say. Enormous disbelief expressed as a noisy clearing of the nostrils.

He had the television on now, and was quarrelling with that. Then he asked if there was anything we'd like to see ourselves. It was the precise moment when I recognised that he was pleased by our being there. I said I'd noticed from the *Radio Times* that a pianist was playing a brief programme of Chopin on the other side. He switched over but at once turned the sound down to a whisper, and was scathing about the fit of the pianist's evening dress. A nocturne was shouted down (I put it to myself, secretly) by a discussion, conducted by my father with himself, of the circumstances in which a white tie should be worn rather than a black one.

Edward Blishen, SHAKY RELATIONS

3   When she was twenty-three years old, she met, at a Christmas party, a young man from the Erewash Valley. Morel was then twenty-seven years old. He was well set-up, erect, and very smart. He had wavy black hair that shone again, and a vigorous black beard that had never been shaved. His cheeks were ruddy, and his red, moist mouth was noticeable because he laughed so often and so heartily. He had that rare thing, a rich, ringing laugh. Gertrude Coppard had watched him, fascinated. He was so full of colour and animation, his voice ran so easily into comic grotesque, he was so ready and so pleasant with everybody. Her own father had a rich fund of humour, but it was satiric. This man's was different: soft, non-intellectual, warm, a kind of gambolling.

She herself was opposite. She had a curious, receptive mind which found much pleasure and amusement in listening to other folk. She was clever in leading folk to talk. She loved ideas, and was considered very intellectual. What she liked most of all was an argument on religion or philosophy or politics with some educated man. This she did not often enjoy. So she always had people tell her about themselves, finding her pleasure so.

In her person she was rather small and delicate, with a large brow, and dropping bunches of brown silk curls. Her blue eyes were very straight, honest, and searching. She had the beautiful hands of the Coppards. Her dress was always subdued. She wore dark blue silk, with a peculiar silver chain of silver scallops. This, and a heavy brooch of twisted gold, was her only ornament. She was still perfectly intact, deeply religious, and full of beautiful candour.

D. H. *Lawrence*, SONS AND LOVERS

B   Find another description of a character and explain how the writer enables you to 'see' and understand that character.

16◆Assumptions

Rita has red hair. Rita has a quick temper. Does that mean that all people with red hair have quick tempers? No. Some people with black hair or blond hair have quick tempers. Some people with red hair are placid and easy-going. Yet the view that all people with red hair have quick tempers is the kind of assumption that some people make. An **assumption** is a view or a statement that people assert to be correct, though it may be based on only a few examples and may not have any logical justification.

Another example is the view that all Welsh people can sing. Is this true? Choral singing may be popular in Wales, but statistically do more Welsh people sing than any other? Are there no Welsh people who are tone deaf?

That example is comparatively harmless, but assumptions of this kind can lead to stereotyping where whole races or classes of people are categorised or labelled as possessing certain qualities or defects because of a few examples or because of prejudice. 'Irish jokes', for instance, spread the idea that all Irish people are stupid.

Do not be taken in by such views. Examine them. See if they make sense. Ask yourself if they are logical. Ask yourself what proof there is. Find examples which show that such statements are false. Do not just accept them because someone says so.

A Look at the following statements and point out the assumptions that are being made. Explain why you think they are assumptions and say what arguments you would use to counter them.

1 Over the last three years, the number of burglaries in this town has been 76, 84 and 92. Next year they will probably number 100.

2 Only three people knew where the missing key was kept, so one of them must have taken it.

3 The average Englishman drinks three pints of beer a week. John Smith is an average Englishman. Therefore he is bound to drink three pints of beer a week.

4 Janet's parents would not allow her to go to the local youth club because they were certain that if she went she would be led astray.

5 The only thing Americans are interested in is making money.

6 Having lost the toss in the last four matches, the captain was certain he would win it next time.

7 Fat people are much more placid than thin people.

8 A: Look at that car. It's all over the place.
   B: Well, what can you expect? It's a woman driver.

9 I don't think students should get grants to go to university. All they do is
   waste their time. I don't see why our taxes should be used to pay for them
   when the nation gets nothing back from them.

10 If it takes four minutes to run one mile, it takes eight minutes to run two
    miles.

B Study the following passage. Point out where assumptions are made and where you
are expected to accept illogical or unsupported statements. How effective are the
arguments given here in favour of the death penalty?

Murderers are cruel sadistic monsters. They must be hanged. What they do
puts them beyond the pale of humanity. They are not humans and therefore
they cannot expect to be treated as humans. They must be made to see the
error of their ways, and the only way of doing that is by hanging them.

British justice is the finest in the world, but by not imposing the death
sentence people will think we are failing to punish crime justly. It is the
principle of justice itself that is at stake. How can we claim to be a just nation
if people who murder are not themselves executed? An eye for an eye and a
tooth for a tooth is the very basis of justice.

Some people claim that hanging is cruel, but it is more humane than the
other penalties at present imposed. It is quick, and thanks to modern
methods, painless. It is only the agitators who campaign against the death
penalty who say it is cruel. The reality is that it is a kindness to the murderer.
Far better to be hanged than to suffer the slow torture of life imprisonment
which is in any case a burden on the long-suffering taxpayer.

There are other objections to life imprisonment. There is the chance that
the murderer may escape. He or she would then be free to murder again. Nor
is life imprisonment what it says. It is only a nominal sentence. In no time at
all the murderer will be released. How can the ordinary person feel safe
knowing that there are murderers on the prowl seeking their next victim?

The crux of the matter is that only hanging acts as a deterrent to
murderers. In the past, many a would-be murderer must have refrained from
committing this heinous crime knowing that such an act would result in
certain execution. Put yourself in his or her shoes. You would not commit
murder knowing that the penalty for so doing was death. It is the same with
murderers.

So-called liberals point to the experience of other European countries where
the death penalty has ceased to exist. But what happens in those countries is
no guide to what may happen here. It is our safety that is at risk, not theirs.
Only the return of the death penalty can ensure that we can sleep safely in our
beds.

17◆Facts and Opinions

Majorca is an island in the Mediterranean

Majorca is the best place to go to for a holiday

Which of these statements is a fact and which is an opinion? How can you tell?

A **fact** is a statement that can be verified by evidence. There is proof (or the possibility of proof) to show that it is correct.

An **opinion** is a statement which may or may not be true. There is insufficient evidence to prove it one way or the other. Often, it is simply the expression of a belief or a feeling.

Sometimes writers pass off opinions as facts in the hope that readers will accept them. We need to be able to distinguish between facts and opinions in what we read so that we can guard against this. When we recognise that a statement is an opinion and not a fact, we need to examine it more carefully. We need to consider whether there is any supporting evidence and how trustworthy the person is who is expressing the opinion. Then we are in a position to make up our own minds.

A Which of the following are facts and which are opinions? Justify your view.

1 Nuclear weapons have ensured peace in the world for the last forty years.

2 The rise in crime is due to increased unemployment.

3 Everyone in this country has an equal opportunity to succeed in life.

4 *The Sun* is a more popular newspaper than the *Morning Star*.

5 Violence on television encourages violence in society.

6 A mile can be run in less than four minutes.

7 Travelling broadens the mind.

8 The postal service is getting worse.

9 Every year, the proportion of old people in the population of this country increases.

10 British is best.

B Write down five statements that are facts and five statements that are opinions.

C Examine the following passages and point out where opinions are being passed off as facts.

1

The only rule in the tarmac jungle is the arrival of the fittest: so cut that cyclist and curse that coach. Louisa Young describes the vicious Highway Code ruling London's mean streets.

WHOSE ROAD IS IT ANYWAY?

The road to hell may be paved with good intentions, but it is the only road that is. Every other road in the country (and particularly in the cities) is paved with evil intentions, evil tempers, evil attitudes and evil manners. 'The road' is one of those places where everybody knows that they are in the right, always. And the other guy is in the wrong. Always. Especially if you're a motor-cyclist and he's a cabby. Or you're a cabby and he's a cyclist. Or you're a cyclist and he's a lorry driver. Or you're a lorry driver and she's a pedestrian. Evil road manners are not so much to do with individuals or individual driving habits but with tribes – it is in fact a sort of tribal warfare, and which tribe you belong to depends on your form of transport at the time. You are how you travel. Each area has variations on the basic tribal system but we hailed a member of each of London's major road tribes and asked them to describe for us the view from their own particular driving seat.

TELEGRAPH SUNDAY MAGAZINE

2

During the last forty years there has been a rapid collapse of religious belief; of morality; of culture and of the arts (it is typical of the way truth is stood on its head that 'The Arts' are commonly said to be flourishing in England as never before); a collapse of law and order; a growth of cruelty and brutality. Our hooligans are now the foremost in Europe. As well as yobbery, we have jobbery; there are circles where to be dishonest and known to be so is no longer a matter for shame. 'Enterprise' and money-making are commended for their own sake. False science, which regards the whole universe, human beings included, as one experimental laboratory, daily extends its empire, here as elsewhere almost unopposed, whether in the field of nuclear power or genetic engineering.

There is another factor, not in itself a moral one, but obviously of great importance. England, until lately a homogeneous nation, has been part-colonised by large numbers of alien and unassimilable people. We are continually told (for the liberal consensus it is a primary article of faith) that whether we like it or not we are now a 'multi-racial and multi-cultural society'. Does anyone really believe it? Such a society has probably never existed in the history of the world. Is it likely to come about in the home of what was once called, without undue embarrassment, 'the island race'?

Peter Simple, TELEGRAPH SUNDAY MAGAZINE

3

It is no good to expect Anglo-Saxon youths to learn by "discovery" or self-guidance. The only way to teach them is by rote, learning things by heart under threat of dire punishment if they fail.

The one thing which has always kept the Brits on the straight and narrow is a certain terror of authority, learned in youth and never quite forgotten. It was that terror which enabled us to become a tolerant, easy-going collection of individuals, when grown-up.

We also retained in later life a certain dislike of authority, carefully hidden, and that was always one of the most delightful characteristics of England, evident right through the community even to the top of official classes who administered it.

Take away that initial terror and hatred of authority, and you are left with a society divided between those who love authority for its own sake—the power maniacs and masochists among us—and those who may resent it slightly but are to all intents and purposes unaware of its existence. These New Brits get no thrill from defying it.

Auberon Waugh,
EVENING STANDARD

18 ◆ Defective Arguments

People do not always play fair when they make a point in an argument. On the other hand, they sometimes think they have made a point when they have not. Here are some of the methods people use to try to get you to accept what they say.

Assertions   making a statement about something and expecting to be believed, although no evidence is provided.

Generalising from personal experience   assuming that what is true of one person's experience is true for all.

Generalising from a specific example   using one example as a basis for making a general rule about all such cases.

Making an emotional or sentimental appeal   trying to influence the argument by appealing to the feelings not the intellect.

Making an appeal to prejudice   dealing in stereotypes and assuming that everyone else accepts those stereotypes.

Unconvincing parallels   using a parallel or illustration which is not directly parallel or relevant.

Hearsay evidence   using what someone else has said as though it were evidence.

Passing off an opinion as a fact   stating that something is a fact when it is only an opinion.

Making an assumption   stating that something is the case when there is incomplete evidence for believing it to be so.

Being illogical   using one point to 'prove' another when there is no logical connection between the two.

Exaggeration   trying to persuade people by overstating a case.

Attacking an opponent's view   abusing, distorting or ridiculing an opponent or an opponent's view without providing real evidence.

A   Here are examples of defective arguments, one for each of the types described. Match each of them with the appropriate definition and explain in your own words why they are defective as arguments.

   1   Anyone who believes in equality of the sexes must support Valerie Davies for the post.

2   Of course, there isn't any doubt about it. Hanging acts as a deterrent.

3   People like that can't be expected to behave any better.

4   If people are allowed to smuggle their pets into the country, it will result in a worse plague than the Black Death.

5   This child has lied to me. I shall never believe anything he ever says to me again.

6   Only a fool would believe that eating carrots helps you to see in the dark.

7   I approve of caning. It never did me any harm.

8   It's not possible for women to be ministers of religion any more than it is for dogs to talk.

9   You can't believe anything you read in the newspapers.

10   My dad says that men are more intelligent than women.

11   When we look at those limpid brown eyes and Bambi-like faces, how can we permit these barbaric methods of raising calves?

12   Elvis Presley was the greatest singer who ever lived.

B   Study the following extract from the play *Twelve Angry Men* by Reginald Rose. The twelve men form the jury which is considering the case of a youth charged with murder. Comment on the kinds of arguments which are put forward and point out where they are defective.

Foreman: Okay. *(To the 7th Juror.)* How about the next gentleman?

7th Juror: Me? *(He pauses, looks around, shrugs and rises.)* I don't know, it's practically all said already. We can talk about it for ever. It is the same thing. I mean, this kid is o for five. Look at his record. He was in the Children's Court when he was ten for throwing a rock at his teacher. At fifteen he was in Reform School. He stole a car. He's been arrested for mugging. He was picked up twice for trying to slash another teenager with a knife. He's real quick with switchknives, they say. This is a very fine boy.

8th Juror: Ever since he was five years old his father beat him up regularly. He used his fists.

7th Juror: So would I. A kid like that. *(He sits.)*

4th Juror: Wouldn't you call those beatings a motive for him to kill his father?

8th Juror *(after a pause):* I don't know. It's a motive for him to be an angry, hostile kid. I'll say that.

3rd Juror: *(moving up L of the table):* It's the kids, the way they are nowadays. Angry! Hostile! You can't do a damn thing with them. Just the way they talk to you. Listen, when I was his age I used to call my father 'Sir'. That's right. Sir! You ever hear a boy call his father that any more?

8th Juror: Fathers don't seem to think it's important any more.

3rd Juror: No? Have you got any kids?

8th Juror: Three.

3rd Juror: *(moving to L of the 8th Juror):* Yeah, well I've got this one, a boy of twenty years old. You know how it is. You bring up kids. You try to do everything for them to make 'em decent. We did everything for that boy and what happened? When he was nine he ran away from a fight. I saw him. I was so ashamed I almost threw up. So I told him right out. 'I'm gonna make a man outa you or I'm gonna bust you in half trying.' Well, I made a man outa him all right. When he was sixteen we had a battle. He hit me in the face. He's big, y'know. I haven't seen him in two years. Rotten kid. You work your heart out . . . *(He breaks off. He has said more than he intended and more passionately than he intended it. He is embarrassed. He looks around at the others. Loudly.)* All right. Let's get on with it. *(He crosses angrily above the table and stands at the window up RC.)*

4th Juror *(rising):* I think we're missing the point here. This boy, let's say he's a product of a filthy neighbourhood and a broken home. We can't help that. We're here to decide whether he's guilty or innocent of murder, not to go into reasons why he grew up this way. He was born in a slum. Slums are breeding grounds for criminals. I know it. So do you. It's no secret. Children from slum backgrounds are potential menaces to society. Now I think . . .

10th Juror *(interrupting):* Brother, you can say that again. The kids who crawl outa those places are real trash. I don't want any part of them, I'm telling you.

(The 5th Juror has reacted to all this. His face is angry as he tries to control himself but his voice shakes as he speaks.)

5th Juror *(rising):* I've lived in a slum all my life . . .

(The 4th Juror sits. The 10th Juror suddenly knows he has said the wrong thing.)

10th Juror *(rising):* Oh, now wait a second . . .

5th Juror *(furiously):* I used to play in a back yard that was filled with garbage.

(The Foreman rises.)

Maybe it still smells on me.

10th Juror *(his anger rising):* Now listen, sonny . . .

Foreman *(to the 5th Juror):* Now let's be reasonable. There's nothing personal . . .

5th Juror *(loudly):* There is something personal! *(He looks around at the others, then suddenly he has nothing to say, clenches his fist and sits.)*

(The 3rd Juror moves to the 5th Juror and pats him on the shoulder. The 5th Juror does not look up.)

Foreman: All right, let's stop all this arguing. We're wasting time here.

Reginald Rose, TWELVE ANGRY MEN

19◆Evaluating an Argument

Much writing is intended to persuade us to accept a particular argument or point of view. Advertisements, editorials, political pamphlets, feature articles in newspapers are examples. As readers, we have to examine writing of this kind carefully, weigh up the points being put forward and decide for ourselves how convincingly the case has been presented.

We have to consider the following:

– whether arguments are supported by evidence

– the nature of that evidence

– whether opinion is passed off as fact (see Chapter 17)

– whether the writer uses defective arguments (see Chapter 18)

– whether arguments against the point of view being presented are deliberately omitted or are dismissed without convincing evidence

– whether the writer is giving only a prejudiced and biased view

– the language and tone used.

It could help to make a list of the main points the writer is making and then see what kind of evidence is given to support these main points.

A Examine the advertisement opposite for the Renault 5 I–D car. What arguments are given for buying this particular car? How persuasive do you find them? Consider the language and tone used and the associations suggested by the imagery. How effective and appropriate do you consider them to be?

IT'S MORE THAN A NEW 5. IT'S A NEW I–D.

Bored with the old image? This is your chance to get a brand new body. In Carmen Red, Silver Grey, White, Midnight Blue or Lakeland Green.

Face a bit pasty? Simply sit inside the new Renault 5 I–D and your skin instantly takes on a deep Mediterranean tan, thanks to the tinted windows.

You can even get that First World War Flying Ace 'wind-in-the-hair' effect with the tilt-up glass sunroof.

This car looks better on than a new wardrobe (brass handles and sharp wooden edges never did much for anyone) and comes with a special edition badging flash.

And for those people who insist that it's what you're like inside that matters, there's the great indoors.

Cheeky seats sport bold blocks of red and green, trimmed with a fine yellow line that just begs to be parked on.

A green and pleasant carpet rolls beneath your feet, and front seats are backed with an intriguing ribbed vinyl finish (always a good conversation starter).

Rear seats split 60/40, so there's always room for the odd friend, and the odd friend's shopping.

Not forgetting the five speed gearbox. And the Philips stereo, which will do more for your ears than that new haircut.

There's even internally adjustable door mirrors for the hopelessly vain. And a choice of 1108cc (3 door) or 1237cc (3 or 5 door) engine.

All from £6000. So be warned. Your bank manager may start to find you attractive.

Visit your local dealer or phone 0800 400 415 (24 hrs/free) for a brochure. All Renault cars have a twelve month unlimited mileage and six year anti-perforation warranty.

THERE'S MORE TO LIFE WITH **RENAULT**

THE RENAULT 5 I–D FROM £6,000 TO £6,455

B In this article, Auberon Waugh gives his views on examinations and continuous assessment. How much evidence does he supply to support his views? What kind of tone does he use? Does this make his arguments more – or less – convincing?

Top marks for exams

IF I WERE still at school and preparing for my new GCSE exams in the summer, I might be tempted to raise a cheer for the National Association of Head Teachers, which has just proposed that all formal examinations for 16-year-olds should be abolished. The National Association suggests they should be replaced by continuous assessment and "broadly based profiles of pupil achievement".

It all sounds quite painless, and definitely preferable to the nightmare of exams.

There is certainly a case to be made against exams. Some people suffer from appalling nerves, which prevents them sitting down to an exam paper unless they are stuffed with tranquillisers, which can scarcely be good for their concentration. Nor do examination results, in all their cruel baldness, take into account such things as effort or family background.

All these disadvantages would be swept away by a system of continuous assessment, where teachers would be sending in reports the whole time. But before we decide to garland our own friendly neighbourhood head teacher in spring flowers and carry him or her around on our shoulders, perhaps we should look at the disadvantages.

Teachers, as most of us have discovered, come in all shapes and sizes. Some are wise, hardworking, conscientious and deeply concerned for their pupils. Others are bad tempered, bossy, unfair, lazy, incompetent, insecure and given to favouritism.

You might suppose that you would be safe in the first group, but even with them there is a danger. The better and more conscientious a teacher, the more he (or she) will bend over backwards to make allowances for a pupil's lack of natural ability, his unfortunate family background, etc.

This is all very well, but it must be boiled down to a simple grading which can be understood by UCCA, the universities' central clearing computer, as well as by future employers, who are not going to wade through 20 pages of educational assessment on every job applicant.

None of these nice, caring teachers is going to give a pupil the sort of grade which condemns him to a life of failure and unemployment, unless there are reasons to suspect him of racism, sexism or something of the sort. But under those circumstances, the system breaks down, because gradings give no idea of genuine ability.

Now let us look at teachers who are less perfect. Where they are idle or incompetent, their assessments are worth nothing. Where they are unfair, or given to strong likes or dislikes among their pupils, the results are even worse. They can use the system to pay off old scores, and condemn a pupil ever after for having once got on the wrong side of them.

Exams, for all their faults, are at least impartial. Unpopular children can do as well at them as popular ones.

The final result of continuous assessment would be an enormous increase in teachers' power. Some might welcome this if it helped them keep better discipline in the classroom, but of course it wouldn't. Disruptive elements would be no more impressed by the thought of future assessments than they are by the present punishments.

Worse than this, a system of continuous assessment would give nobody the chance to judge how well a school was keeping up its standards.

Auberon Waugh
JUNIOR GUARDIAN

C In this article, Yvonne Roberts comments on a case in which the headmaster of a private school who caned a pupil for getting low marks in an examination was found not guilty of assaulting the pupil. What arguments does the writer use to attack the verdict and to oppose corporal punishment? What evidence does she bring forward to support her views? What kind of language and tone does she use? Do you think she makes a convincing case?

The weals of justice

YVONNE ROBERTS hits back at a legal judgment in favour of corporal punishment

ON MONDAY, we had a victory for institutionalised violence when John Pearman, head of Friern Barnet Grammar School, was acquitted of assaulting Barry Tavner, 13, whom he caned five times because he failed to do well in his exams.

A year ago today, ironically, the House of Commons voted to end flogging in state schools. From August 17, parents may sue a teacher for damages. Fortunately for Mr John Pearman, independent schools are exempt: wallops on the fees will still be permitted.

In Mr Pearman's case, the judge, Christopher Hordern, QC, was obviously not unfamiliar with the sound of swishing bamboo himself. He jokily advised the court on how to treat bruised buttocks.

"Never heard of Pomade de Vin?" he said. "Absolutely invaluable for bruises and grazes."

If a judge had handed out such advice to an elderly victim of an identical beating, it would have been considered unforgivable. Violence on the syllabus – *taught* violence – however, is altogether more acceptable; for this judge, quite a jape, in fact. No wonder the young are confused.

After the court case, Mr Pearman pronounced: "It is a good judgment for the education world at large." What nonsense. It is a good judgment for a Victorian society which should long since be defunct.

Under-achieving

It's a society in which adults have the right to do what they wish with children simply because they hold Authority.

The flood of reported cases of child sex abuse shows how this principle can be challenged – and how vicious the adult backlash becomes when power is questioned.

John Pearman administered the beating not because Barry Tavner had been badly behaved – but because he was "under-achieving".

The headmaster obviously hasn't done his homework. Only last month, a report by Her Majesty's Inspectors condemned corporal punishment. Why? Because as an educational tool, it fails. It fails to keep discipline. It fails to raise academic standards.

Courtesy and high standards "cannot be achieved by coercive and repressive measures", the inspectors state, using surveys of schools over 10 years.

Under-achievement is frequently caused by a multitude of reasons (domestic upheavals, for instance). Even if the cause is plain laziness, does it really merit a punishment which eats into a child's life for a whole year, as it did for Barry?

This is the kind of tactic much loved by adults who believe childhood is not to be enjoyed but endured; a necessary gauntlet of pain.

Mr Pearman is only 38, a young man with an antiquated vision. The other reason he caned Barry, according to a policeman who gave evidence, was that he felt the boy's under-achievement might be due to "the lack of a man around the house".

Single mother

Mrs Theresa Tavner is a widow, a single parent (who sees no need to beat her children). Mr Pearman, in his arrogance, assumes that a woman alone cannot cope, that to function properly, every household needs a man.

Ultimately, Mr Pearman is to be pitied. If education is a continuous process, his development has been stunted by his addiction to a stagnant society. The wonder is that some parents pay him in spite of that.

LONDON DAILY NEWS

20 ◆ The Writer's Attitude – Irony

Usually writers make their attitudes or their points of view clear. They tell the reader in direct straightforward statements – for example:

> It is time the government did something to improve the state of the roads in this country.

Or else they colour their words to make their attitudes clear. (See chapter 6.)

But sometimes writers disguise their attitudes or points of view. The reader has to interpret what is being said in order to understand the meaning that lies underneath. Because the reader has to work at it, the point is made more powerfully. The reader can feel flattered at sharing a kind of secret or a private joke with the writer.

Some of the ways in which writers can disguise their attitudes are:

- by treating something serious as though it were comic

- by pretending to support a point of view when they are in fact undermining it

- by taking an argument to extreme lengths in order to show that the basic argument is unsound

- by treating something with exaggerated seriousness in order to show how trivial it is.

The weapon most commonly used in writing of this kind is **irony**. Irony is a device whereby writers say the opposite of what they mean or something different from what they mean in order to give their real meaning more emphasis. For instance, Jane Austen wrote in a letter:

> Mr Richard Harvey is going to be married, but it is a great secret and only known to half the neighbourhood, so you must not mention it.

Jane Austen is pretending that the marriage is 'a great secret' when it is clear that it is not. She is probably making fun of the way the family tried to keep the marriage a secret and failed.

There is a danger with irony that readers accept the literal or surface meaning and fail to realise that the real meaning is hidden underneath. You have to look for the clues (what clues are there in the extract by Jane Austen given above?) and ask yourself, 'Is this really what the writer means?'

Clues include:

- the use of a tone that is 'tongue in cheek'

- deliberate exaggeration

- absurd statements that are treated as though they are perfectly ordinary

- the assumption that everyone believes something which is very dubious.

A What are the attitudes and points of view of the three writers in the following? How can you tell?

1

Children's TV diet

In last week's issue you published a letter complaining about cartoon characters in children's programmes smoking. I feel this letter does not go quite far enough. Characters in children's programmes are frequently seen carrying out all manner of potentially hazardous occupations such as walking down the street, riding bicycles and eating sweets. Indeed, the mother in a recent programme was heard to say that she had given her son crisps and a bar of chocolate in his lunch box. Any nutritionist will tell you that such a diet can have very harmful long-term effects on children.

Perhaps it would be more acceptable to some people if all children's programmes were replaced with a blank screen – unless, of course, you happen to agree with my eight-year-old son who says, 'Just because people on television do a thing, it doesn't mean that I have to do it.'

Letter in a magazine

2

I DON'T see why anyone should be so up in arms about the new Bill to curb trades union powers. After all, it only says that all trade unions must hold a secret ballot on whether or not to strike, and that whatever the result nobody needs to take any notice of it.

This is exactly the same principle that the late Sir David Owen invoked when the majority of the SDP voted to merge with the Liberal Party. Sir David simply pointed out that the majority who voted to merge could, while those who voted not to, needn't.

It's a principle I should very much like to see extended to General Elections. No matter which party the majority votes for, nobody should be compelled to take any notice of the result. If you didn't vote for a Conservative government, you shouldn't be compelled to have one. Those who voted Labour could have a Labour government, and those who voted Liberal could have an SDP one.

It's what Norman Fowler, the Employment Secretary, calls giving people "protection from the abuse of power and the rights they are entitled to expect in a free society." Of course, he was only thinking about trades union members, but the wider application of the principle is clear. We need to give the Government of this country back to the people.

If it is wrong for a trades unionist to be forced to do something he doesn't want to simply because the majority have voted for it, why should any individual be forced to do anything they didn't vote for?

I, myself, for example, didn't vote for stopping at red traffic lights at the last election. So why shouldn't I have the freedom to go on red lights and stop at green ones, if that's what I choose to do?

Terry Jones, JUNIOR GUARDIAN

3

In Westminster Abbey

Let me take this other glove off
  As the *vox humana* swells,
And the beauteous fields of Eden
  Bask beneath the Abbey bells.
Here, where England's statesmen lie,
Listen to a lady's cry.

Gracious Lord, oh bomb the Germans.
  Spare their women for Thy Sake,
And if that is not too easy
  We will pardon Thy Mistake.
But, gracious Lord, whate'er shall be,
Don't let anyone bomb me.

Keep our Empire undismembered
  Guide our Forces by Thy Hand,
Gallant blacks from far Jamaica,
  Honduras and Togoland;
Protect them Lord in all their fights,
And, even more, protect the whites.

Think of what our Nation stands for,
  Books from Boots and country lanes,
Free speech, free passes, class distinction,
  Democracy and proper drains.
Lord, put beneath Thy special care
One-eighty-nine Cadogan Square.

Although dear Lord I am a sinner,
  I have done no major crime;
Now I'll come to Evening Service
  Whensoever I have the time.
So, Lord, reserve for me a crown.
And do not let my shares go down.

I will labour for Thy Kingdom,
  Help our lads to win the war,
Send white feathers to the cowards
  Join the Women's Army Corps,
Then wash the Steps around Thy Throne
In the Eternal Safety Zone.

Now I feel a little better,
  What a treat to hear Thy Word,
Where the bones of leading statesmen,
  Have so often been interr'd.
And now, dear Lord, I cannot wait
Because I have a luncheon date.

John Betjeman

21 ◆ Summarising

The purpose of summarising is to extract the main points from a piece of writing and present them in a form that is briefer and more easily accessible. Secretaries may summarise an article for a busy employer. Newspapers may summarise a report for the benefit of their readers. Students may summarise a chapter in a book to help them with their revision.

Here are suggestions about how to set about making a summary:

- Read the passage in order to get a general impression of what it is about.

- Read the passage again, this time concentrating on the main points the writer is making.

- Jot down the main points – in tabulated form if you like.

- Using your notes, write a piece of continuous prose that incorporates these main points. As far as possible use your own words. Try to make your writing flow from one point to another, perhaps by using linking words or phrases like 'moreover', 'for this reason', 'in spite of this', 'however', 'even so'.

- Keep firmly to the points made in the passage. Do not add any ideas or opinions of your own.

- Count the number of words in your summary if a specific number is stated. If you have too many words, see where you can cut some by expressing a point more concisely. If you have not used enough words, read the passage again to see if you have omitted something important.

A Make a summary of the following account of the Race Relations Acts, using about 180 words.

Race Relations Acts

There was much open discrimination against black immigrants in the 1950s and '60s. Notices saying "NO COLOURED" were familiar outside private rented housing and other places.

In 1965 the first Race Relations Act was passed. This made it unlawful to discriminate against people because of their colour, race or national origin in such public places as restaurants, pubs, cinemas, swimming pools and public transport. The Act also said it was an offence to stir up hatred against a minority group. A Race Relations Board was set up to receive complaints from individuals about discrimination. This Board could enquire into cases and try to reach agreement between parties.

Another Act was passed in 1968. This made discrimination illegal also in most cases of housing, employment and advertising. The 1968 Act also set up the Community Relations Commission to work for better racial harmony. The Commission pressed the government for stronger measures to prevent discrimination and punish those who break the law.

A third Race Relations Act followed in 1976, to make the law against discrimination stronger still. This Act increased the legal protection of minorities in such areas as jobs, housing and education. "Racial discrimination" was widened to include *indirect* discrimination (where conditions or requirements are set which have the effect of keeping out some racial groups without good reason). Another of the changes was to bring clubs into the scope of the law. It became illegal for a club of more than 25 members to refuse membership on the grounds of colour or race.

The new 1976 Act also helped individual complaints. Under the old Act, every complaint went to the Race Relations Board. The 1976 Act gave individuals direct access to the courts. Complaints about jobs go directly to an industrial court called a tribunal. Victims may be awarded financial compensation and given a recommended course of action to put things right. Other complaints (on housing, etc) go to county courts. Damages may be awarded, including awards for injured feelings, and an order against the discrimination.

Another aspect of the 1976 Act is that it allows and encourages local education authorities to take special steps to help minorities.

There are some situations not covered by the 1976 Act. For example, it is *not* against the law to discriminate on racial grounds for employment in a private house. It is also *not* unlawful to discriminate where the characteristics of a particular racial group are a genuine qualification for the job (for example, Chinese waiter wanted for Chinese restaurant). It is also *not* against the law to discriminate on racial grounds in disposing of premises where a landlord or a near relative of the landlord lives on the premises. Discrimination is also allowed on racial grounds for fostering children, or for care of children or others in a private house.

Each of the Race Relations Acts has been a step towards the aim that all people in Britain should have equality of opportunity regardless of the colour of their skin, or where they are from. Of course, laws are made to control what people do, not what people feel or think. However, laws do have an effect on public attitudes. By discouraging racial prejudice in what people *do*, the law is also making *attitudes* of prejudice less acceptable.

Nance Lui Fyson, MULTI-ETHNIC BRITAIN

B   Read the following newspaper article. Make a summary of the main points, using about 150 words.

Children are told to give up chips

A LEADING medical expert warned today that the diet of British schoolchildren needs to be radically changed for the sake of their future health.

Professor Barry Lewis, head of the Department of Chemical Pathology at St Thomas's Hospital, was commenting on a nutritional survey carried out in 1983 involving more than 3200 children aged from 10 to 15.

It found that despite medical advice over the past decade, children were dependent on nutrients from chips, cakes and biscuits—producing a diet heavily overloaded with fat.

A report on the survey, commissioned by the Department of Health and Social Security, was carried today by a national newspaper, although it remains officially unpublished.

Professor Lewis, who is a leading exponent of healthy eating, said: "The diet of young people is exactly the opposite of what we would recommend.

"I cannot say they are harming their arteries, although we know that artery diseases begin very early in life. But they are establishing food preferences which are going to be hard to break."

Professor Lewis said he would like to see fundamental changes in British dietary patterns to reduce our high rate of heart disease and stroke (following hardening of the arteries).

The recommendations, which have been endorsed by the World Health Organisation, include reducing intakes of saturated fat and increasing fibre-rich foods like fruit and vegetables.

Habits

Professor Lewis said: "I accept that it is going to take a long time to educate the population and it is easy to castigate the authorities for being slow to respond to the advice.

"Moreover, heart disease mortality is beginning to fall among young adults, although the total number of deaths has not changed.

"I am sad about our children establishing bad dietary habits. I think the situation could be improved if dietary advice was provided in schools and if parents gave a better example.

"I would also like to see the manufacturers of wholesome foods promoting the products more energetically."

The DHSS report found that nearly all the children in the survey consumed potato chips and other potato products, cakes and biscuits.

It says: "Because of the large quantity of chips, cakes and biscuits consumed by these schoolchildren, the consumption of most other food items was correspondingly reduced."

Alan Massam, EVENING STANDARD

22◆Reading for Information

When reading a piece of writing, we may not necessarily be interested in everything that is being said. For instance, in an article about various school systems, we may be interested only in what it has to say about comprehensive schools. We would therefore skim through the article until we came to specific sections dealing with comprehensive schools and then read those sections with greater attention. This is called reading for information. The purpose is to isolate and concentrate only on those areas of the piece of writing which supply the information we are looking for.

Here is how to set about it:

– Read the passage in order to get a general impression of what it is about.

– Make sure you understand the task that has been set, that is, the information you want to extract from the passage.

– Read the passage again, keeping in mind all the time the information you want. Isolate the sections of the passage which provide this information.

– Jot down the points from these sections – in tabulated form if you like – ignoring anything that does not relate to the information you are seeking.

– Use your notes to write a piece of continuous prose that incorporates these notes. As far as possible use your own words. Try to make your writing flow from one point to another, perhaps by using linking words or phrases like 'on the other hand', 'nevertheless', 'secondly', 'also', 'another reason . . .'

A Using only the information found in the article opposite, explain how dogs react to heat, how best to ensure that they are not affected by heat, and what to do if they are affected by heat.

It's really a dog's life in the heat

My family has just returned from our annual holiday. Unfortunately for us we arrived in one of the Greek islands the day the freak heat wave started and we were very uncomfortable in temperatures of 115° and very high humidity.

As you know these very high temperatures were most unusual in the area and indeed many people died as a result of heat-related problems.

I was interested to see how pets coped in these extreme conditions; they did all the sensible things that sometimes holiday-makers didn't.

For example, in the heat of the day (which lasted about 12 hours) dogs and cats could be seen flat out in the shade of a tree, snoozing the day peacefully away, expending no energy and keeping as cool as possible.

They would only shift to follow the shade as the sun moved, or unless disturbed by vacationers walking or running about.

I was quite surprised when I returned to our cool weather to find that, even in the low temperature summer we are having this year, we have already seen our first cases of heatstroke in dogs, and indeed there are some cases reported in the Veterinary Record this week.

Dogs do not sweat to lose heat as we do; they lose heat by panting and through the soles of their feet.

In warm weather, long-coated dogs can overheat easily especially when running in the sun or when confined in a car.

Heatstroke does not only affect long-coated dogs, however, and in fact is commonest I think in the West Highland Terrier.

Modern cars do have a vast area of glass and when dogs are left in the car, even in very mild weather such as we are now experiencing, there is a greenhouse effect and the heat builds up quickly, the dog starts to pant to lose heat, panting warms up the car even further and the whole problem escalates.

Eventually the owners return and find their pet in great distress; usually just in the early stages of heatstroke with acute rapid panting and possible semi-collapse, but if the dog has been left too long, you may find the dog collapsed, having fits, or even, of course, dead.

Treatment is first to cool the patient as quickly as possible — and body temperature may have risen as high as 109° — and this can be done by any convenient means such as hosing the dog with cold water, or even using ice, or in an emergency even packing frozen food around the patient.

We also need to use drugs to combat the shock and respiratory problems causes by heatstroke.

Heatstroke is a potentially fatal problem which can be easily avoided by taking simple precautions; don't run dogs — especially long-coated varieties — in the sun or in heat but rather exercise them in the cooler morning and evening.

Most importantly — don't ever leave a dog in a parked car in the sun.

Park in the shade (and remember the shade moves) and always leave windows open for ventilation.

Do pop back to the car frequently to check your pet is all right.

If you suspect heatstroke take your dog to your veterinary surgeon as quickly as possible — this is a problem that should be treated as an emergency.

Geoffrey Paradise, BARNET PRESS

B Study these ten paragraphs from a newspaper article, which have been printed in the wrong order. Decide what you think is a reasonable order and list the numbers of the extracts in your new order. Then write an account of the differences between football matches in the 1930s and football matches today, basing it on the information in this article. You should aim to use about 100 words.

1

A red army will be invading Sussex tomorrow, a fact that has already caused some consternation among those who might get caught up in its boisterous path.

2

By any reckoning Arsenal are a great club and Brighton will be out to play David to their Goliath. The Gunners have never been out of the First Division and their history is littered with trophies and records.

3

It was the golden age of football, a time when cup ties were played in a spirit of carnival; supporters displayed their colours with pride without fear of assault or abuse. Some pretty basic remarks were exchanged but they were usually taken in good part. And the terraces were notable for a certain pawky humour which is rare now although happily traces of it still linger on.

4

Times have certainly changed. These days with a match like tomorrow's all-ticket tie, the local police chief has to be nearly as much involved as the clubs' managers. On this occasion it is anticipated that something like 10,000 North Londoners will head for Sussex, most via the A23. Because of the accommodation problems and potential for serious public disorder, the police have insisted that visiting fans should stand on the east terraces and the usual visitors end be transferred to home supporters.

5

The invasion of the reds has nothing to do with the Russians but comes to us in the name of sport for Arsenal and thousands of the club's mighty following of fans are heading for Sussex where they have an important date at the Goldstone ground in the fourth round of the FA Cup. Whatever the result it should be a memorable day in the annals of Sussex sport, provided that a minority of hooligans are prevented from wrecking it.

6

Hooligans cost England its place in European competition but the indications now are that if the game can survive the next six months wthout serious trouble the door could be grudgingly opened to them again.

7

When the clubs met for a cup tie in the 1930s Arsenal's legendary team was peppered with names like Hapgood, Drake, Hulme and Bastin. Ten of their players were England regulars, the other solitary fellow played for Wales.

8

In most matey fashion the teams trained together at the Goldstone for a week before the match which Arsenal duly won 2-0. On the big day there were no outbreaks of aggro. Young fans were not frisked by the law as they came into the ground, there were no barking police dogs and no helicopter hovered above spying for signs of trouble.

9

A considerable police presence should ensure a trouble-free match, after all closed-circuit television has already gone a considerable way towards singling out the trouble-makers inside football grounds. It is what happens outside them that causes concern and will be the reason why certain pubs and shops will be closed tomorrow. 'Past experience has taught me that I just cannot afford to open,' said one rueful landlord.

10

Which is why genuine lovers of football will be praying for good behaviour tomorrow both inside the Goldstone and on the streets and highways outside the ground.

MID SUSSEX TIMES

23◆*Comparing Different Versions*

Writers can interpret or present the same events in different ways. It may simply be a difference in the kind of language used to describe the events or it may go deeper than that. There may be a deliberate attempt to describe the events so as to influence the reader to take a particular point of view.

In newspapers, for instance, reports can be presented in a biased way. Factors you need to examine to determine the degree of bias are:

- the prominence or otherwise given to the report

- the amount of space devoted to it

- the use of photographs

- the size and wording of the headlines

- the facts given and the facts omitted

- the particular emphasis given

- the kind of language used and the tone

- the degree to which opinion is mixed with fact

- the evidence called on to support a view.

A   Compare the captions on the following page which accompanied a photograph of a smiling Mrs Thatcher holding up a large turkey decked with ribbon and holly. The photograph was similar in each case. Do not allow your personal opinions to influence your views.

1 36-POUNDER FOR MAGGIE   Mrs Thatcher was presented with a 36 lb turkey today by Mr Tony Burlton, an executive member of the British Turkey Association.

   Although the Prime Minister planned to give away several turkeys this Christmas to people in her Finchley constituency, she will cook this one herself at Chequers, her country residence.

EVENING STANDARD (page 1)

2 MAGGIE'S GETTING THE BIRD   Maggie Thatcher gets the bird yesterday – and she's delighted with it. The 36 lb turkey was presented to her outside Number 10 by Tony Burlton, a boss of the British Turkey Federation.

   Mrs Thatcher plans to give several turkeys away this year. But she will cook this one herself at Chequers.

THE SUN (page 8)

3 YOU CAN ALL GET STUFFED   You'll all guess the identity of the well-wrapped figure about to enter 10 Downing Street . . . cold, hard to handle but slickly packaged.

   Yes, of course, it's a turkey – a whopping 36 pounder presented to Premier Margaret Thatcher yesterday by British Turkey Federation chief Tony Burlton.

   And she's holding on to it, to take down to Chequers and cook for her Christmas dinner.

DAILY MIRROR (page 7)

4 HEAVYWEIGHT GIFT   Margaret Thatcher struggles to hold a 36 lb turkey which she plans to cook for Christmas lunch at Chequers. The bird is an annual gift from the British Turkey Federation.

THE INDEPENDENT (page 2)

B   Compare the following two accounts of a debate in the House of Commons.

1

MPs Squabble over War Toys

All the child psychologists in the House of Commons had the time of their lives today during a private members' debate calling for a ban on war toys. Mrs Anne Kerr, mover of the motion, was not pulling her punches. She jolted the house on to its toes by telling members that this might be the last time they would be able to discuss the question of violence before the Third World War broke out.

This was pretty rough stuff, said Mr Quintin Hogg, who declared that he did not feel much safer after the honourable lady had put her proposals for survival. After this splendid start she had produced 'an extraordinarily small brown mouse'.

The word 'ban' was the excuse, Mr Hogg said, for much of the woolliest thinking that went on in the Commons, and he continued on a course that came pretty close to demanding a ban on Mrs Kerr.

This motion reflected a very common frame of mind, the member for St Marylebone said. Because we could not control adults or perhaps ourselves, the reaction was to take it out on the children. He was not going to become an apostle of the permissive society but he felt that the Third World War was not going to be stopped by a ban on toy soldiers and imitation tommy-guns.

Mrs Kerr denounced the Government for not producing the Minister for Disarmament to answer her case. In the event, she had to put up with Mr Darling from the Board of Trade, who gave her a very dusty answer and spoke of the 'sensitive social conscience' of the British toy industry.

Taking a leaf out of the Duke's book, Mr Darling told Mrs Kerr that you could not go around banning toy imports for moral or social reasons. Why, somebody might do the same to us.

Mrs Kerr told how her mother had been out shopping for her. She had brought back flame-throwers, bombs and booby-traps. The Kerr homestead was full of these horrifying things. Her hairdresser and the Jehovah's Witnesses were all sure the world was coming to an end.

She took neither of these very seriously – the Commons sighed with relief at this – but there seemed to be a general feeling that we were not long for this world. Her hairdresser's boy friend had failed to keep a date and then on one occasion when he did turn up, he stole her money. It was apparently all to do with war toys and in particular the orgy of them we had every Christmas.

Mr John Tilney, from the Conservative benches, tried to console her. Mankind was naturally pugnacious, he said. Just look what happened at church fêtes; civilized people paying sixpence to break crockery.

Mr Cranley Onslow was very stern with Mrs Kerr; a muddled and misconceived motion, he said. You might as well outlaw golliwogs, cowboys and Indians, Grimm's Fairy Tales or cops and robbers.

Hugh Noyes, THE TIMES

2️⃣ **Ban War Toys, says Mrs Kerr**

Labour MP Mrs Anne Kerr (Rochester and Chatham) called for a ban on the sale, manufacture, import, export and advertisement of what she called 'war' toys in the Commons yesterday.

Moving a resolution to this effect, she said, 'My mother has gone round toy shops and has bought me an armoury of modern war toys which I think are absolutely horrifying.'

Every Christmas she said, was a 'war-toy orgy'. We should not try to impress upon children our own acceptance of violence.

Export Market

Mr George Darling, Minister of State, Board of Trade, said that last year £16 million worth of British toys were exported overseas. The UK toy industry produced some war toys, both for the home and export markets.

'To ban imports for strictly moral or social reasons, which would have to be proved, might well invite retaliatory action against our own exports,' he said.

MORNING STAR

C Find examples of different reports of the same events in different newspapers and comment on how the versions differ.

D Compare the language and effect of these two versions of an extract from the Bible. Which do you prefer and why?

1️⃣

And now I will show you the best way of all.

I may speak in tongues of men or of angels, but if I am without love, I am a sounding gong or a clanging cymbal. I may have the gift of prophecy, and know every hidden truth; I may have faith strong enough to move mountains; but if I have no love, I am nothing. I may dole out all I possess, or even give my body to be burnt, but if I have no love, I am none the better.

Love is patient; love is kind and envies no one. Love is never boastful, nor conceited, nor rude; never selfish, not quick to take offence. Love keeps no score of wrongs; does not gloat over other men's sins, but delights in the truth. There is nothing love cannot face; there is no limit to its faith, its hope and its endurance.

Love will never come to an end. Are there prophets? their work will be over. Are there tongues of ecstasy? they will cease. Is there knowledge? it will vanish away; for our knowledge and our prophecy alike are partial, and the partial vanishes when wholeness comes. When I was a child, my speech, my outlook and my thought were all childish. When I grew up, I had finished with childish things. Now we see only puzzling reflections in a mirror, but then we shall see face to face. My knowledge now is partial; then it will be whole, like God's knowledge of me. In a word, there are three things that last for ever: faith, hope and love; but the greatest of them all is love.

First Letter of Paul to the Corinthians xiii, 1–13,
THE NEW ENGLISH BIBLE, 1970

2

... and yet shew I unto you a more excellent way.

Though I speak with the tongues of men and of angels, and have not charity, I am become as sounding brass, or a tinkling cymbal.

And though I have the gift of prophecy, and understand all mysteries, and all knowledge; and though I have all faith, so that I could remove mountains, and have not charity, I am nothing.

And though I bestow all my goods to feed the poor, and though I give my body to be burned, and have not charity, it profiteth me nothing.

Charity suffereth long, and is kind; charity envieth not; charity vaunteth not itself, is not puffed up,

Doth not behave itself unseemly, seeketh not her own, is not easily provoked, thinketh no evil;

Rejoiceth not in iniquity, but rejoiceth in the truth;

Beareth all things, believeth all things, hopeth all things, endureth all things.

Charity never faileth: but whether there be prophecies, they shall fail; whether there be tongues, they shall cease; whether there be knowledge, it shall vanish away.

For we know in part, and we prophesy in part.

But when that which is perfect is come, then that which is in part shall be done away.

When I was a child, I spoke as a child, I understood as a child, I thought as a child: but when I became a man, I put away childish things.

For now we see through a glass, darkly; but then face to face: now I know in part; but then shall I know even as also I am known.

And now abideth faith, hope, charity, these three; but the greatest of these is charity.

First Epistle of Paul to the Corinthians xiii, 1–13,
AUTHORISED VERSION OF THE BIBLE, 1611

24 ◆ A Range of Material

You may have to read through a range of material in order to see all sides of a question and reach your own conclusions. For instance, if you were writing an essay about *Macbeth*, you would, of course, read the play, but you might also read a biographical note on William Shakespeare and refer to a number of critical commentaries on the play. You would decide what was relevant to your purpose and weigh up one piece against another.

The following process is suggested when looking at a range of material:

- Read it through to get a general impression.

- Make sure you understand the particular purpose for which you are reading.

- Read the material again, identifying and isolating points that are relevant to this purpose. It could help to make notes at particular stages of your reading.

- Make sure you understand how you are to present the information you have selected.

- Write your account, making sure you use language and tone appropriate for the material and the audience addressed.

A Examine the following material which all relates to the police.

   1   is a review of some television programmes about the police

   2   is a recruiting advertisement for the police

   3   is the speech made by Sir David McNee, then Commissioner of the Metropolitan Police, at the funeral of a policeman killed while on duty.

   i   Describe briefly the impression of the police given in each extract.

   ii Comment on the convincingness of each view by evaluating the supporting evidence.

   iii Sum up your own view of the police and the extent to which you agree and/or disagree with the impressions given in this material.

1

The police and the people

Sarah Hollis's parents live in Sudbury where her father is rector. "Their initial reaction was that I must have provoked them, because this is not the way policemen behave." A medical student, involuntarily caught up in the disturbances during Leon Britten's visit to Manchester in 1985, Sarah had been assaulted by the police and subsequently harassed to prevent her giving evidence against them. Her story, told on Central Television's **Reasonable Force** (ITV, July 28), eventually convinced her parents. Up to then, their idea of the way policemen behave was probably not based on much contact with them in working hours.

Same channel, same evening. **The Bill** is a realistic, "police procedural" series. This episode started with a fatal traffic accident. The Bill had to clear up the mess and inform relatives of the victims. They discovered that the crash had been caused by a defective sports car, sold by a fraudulent dealer. We followed the two overlapping storylines: coping with the aftermath of the tragedy, hunting down the villain.

By the time he was found, working with his mates on another illegal vehicle, our sympathies were deeply engaged on the side of the police. We had seen these ordinary coppers trying to tell a woman that her son had been killed and we were involved in their efforts to unravel the cause of his death. Instead of submitting to arrest, the villains tried to escape and were forcibly brought down. It is a cliché of the crime series. The arresting officer lets his feelings run away with him. He is restrained by his colleagues: "Okay, Jack. That's enough. Cut it out."

What we are not led to expect in these fictions about police work, is that the head hitting the car bonnet will belong to an innocent passer-by, that the other officers will join in or that they will perjure themselves to protect a guilty colleague. We are not told of a man blinded while in police custody or a community worker severely assaulted while trying to prevent a riot. There are no strip searches, humiliating questions, threats of reprisals and systematic harassment of witnesses. Our image of the British bobby has changed since the days of *PC49* and *Dixon of Dock Green*, but we are still told that he stands in the front line of the struggle for justice. Some young people and some members of ethnic minorities have low expectations of the police, but the majority of the population believe that, when it comes down to it, the police share the values of their hardhitting but honest counterparts on the screen.

They are happy to reinforce that image. "I expect a higher standard of behaviour from police officers than from the public": Peter Imbert, newly-appointed Commissioner of the Met, was interviewed on **News at Ten** (ITV, July 30) and profiled on **Newsnight** (BBC2, July 31). A "copper's copper", not a "theorist", he is admired for his handling of the Balcombe Street siege and remembered as the Chief Constable in the Thames Valley who, in 1981, allowed the BBC to film the documentary series *Police*. Like *The Bill*, it showed ordinary people working under considerable pressure.

Reasonable Force began with a statement by its producer David Jones: "I believe that the majority of British police officers do a difficult and at times dangerous job with exemplary courage, courtesy and honesty." The programme was about a minority and "about the failure of their fellow officers to bring them to justice".

You could easily miss the implication of the last sentence. The programme centred on a few, exceptional cases of unprovoked violence, most of which, tested in court, had resulted in compensation. It did not argue that such behaviour is common, but it did imply that, when it occurs, there is a general tendency by the force to protect the offenders. We heard from solicitors whose respect for the uniform had suffered and from a former officer who stated bluntly: "You cannot report other policemen and remain in the job." We heard of officers being present at beatings, "lying through their teeth", arrogantly changing their stories in court and never being charged with perjury. Between 1981 and 1985, the Met paid out £500,000 in damages to victims of police violence. One officer was disciplined.

The programme insisted that we are right to demand higher standards of the police, because our democracy relies on it. The official response, when challenged on specific cases, is not reassuring. Chief Constable David Hall: "We're accepting in this discussion about this hypothetical incident, to a degree . . . that it's true. I'm saying that, if it's true, it's quite wrong . . . If it was true, it would surprise me." Or Deputy Assistant Commissioner Peter Winship: "Police officers are rarely charged with perjury because I like to believe that they don't frequently tell lies under oath." That is part of the trouble, and the reason we sometimes need to adjust our image of the Bill.

Robin Buss, THE TIMES EDUCATIONAL SUPPLEMENT

At an average first division match, there are thirty thousand supporters and just one hundred and fifty police. How does a young copper cope; outnumbered two hundred to one?

Photographs by Don McCullin

Y ou're 23 years old. You're a copper on football duty at a West Ham/QPR match. You're in the stands at the "South Bank" end. To your left, behind a wall of wire mesh, the West Ham fans; to your right, the QPR supporters. After a while, you notice that many of the fans aren't watching the game at all. They're watching the other team's fans. When they're not watching you, that is.

If the fans on either side charge as a mob, the fence won't stop them. You have six fellow officers no more than 15 yards away and a personal radio buzzing in your ear. West Ham score. One half of the crowd erupts. The roar's deafening. At the other end, silence.

Crowd swells. The goal's disallowed. Uproar. The slanging match begins. The "blind" referee is no longer the subject of abuse, it's the rival fans. Objects fly overhead. A colleague steps in to escort a drunken troublemaker out. Two more officers step in to help. They carry him, kicking and punching, out of the ground.

Above: The Met's high-tech "Hoolivan" crowd control mobile unit.

Right: The "South Bank" show: The crowd at Upton Park.

YOU'LL NEVER WALK ALONE

Now, instead of six officers around you, there are just three. A scuffle breaks out behind you. Two kids, aged no more than 15, are at each other's throats. One suddenly produces a Stanley knife he's smuggled through the turn-stiles. A quick call on your radio and you're in touch with the 150 plus officers present. Within a few seconds, a dozen of them can be with you.

You're also in contact with the control room in the ground and with what the Fleet Street boys term the "Hoolivan". Both bristle with hi-technology. With long range cameras, video recorders and monitors on board, they can pin-point potential trouble-spots, identify suspects, etc and convey the information to you immediately.

"A kid aged 15 suddenly produces a Stanley knife"

You'll be able to call in "India 99" a Bell 222 helicopter with on-board TV cameras capable of spotting the ringleaders in a crowd from 1,000 feet up.

But for those few seconds before help arrives, you'll have to employ the disarming techniques, arm, wrist and finger locks you'll have been taught at the Police Training School. Back to the match and the off-pitch competitors: you disarm the youth cleanly, safely and using no more force than is necessary. Can you imagine the headlines tomorrow should he break an arm resisting arrest?

Rest assured, when you emerge from your training, you'll be well able to cope after 20 weeks of intensive mind and body building, followed by two years further training, in the station and on the streets.

You'll be taught about the law. The role of the police in London. The responsibilities you'll carry. The way people from all sorts of backgrounds and cultures behave.

Much of an officer's day is spent observing, noting, collating information.

If you're interviewing a suspect, for example, how do you know if he's telling the truth? You'll be taught the rudiments of body language. Gesticulation and feet movements that indicate stress and nervousness. Guilt? Would you be able to spot a drug pusher? A pick-pocket? You'll be taught how to cope with violence. How to restrain someone stronger than yourself. How to deal with bomb scares. How to deal with young glue-sniffers.

For many of the incidents you'll come across, there are no rules just guidelines. How best to inform a wife her husband's been killed, for example. You'll have to find the compassion and tact from within yourself. You'll have to trust your judgement and take action as you see fit.

In all cases you'll have experienced officers on hand or at the other end of your radio, to give advice and help. We can't expect a young officer never to make mistakes. We're not looking for supermen or wonderwomen, nor indeed, Dempseys and Makepeaces.

When we accept a man or woman into the Force (and bear in mind that only one in six applicants makes the grade) we look for a multitude of qualities. In our book, although we value good academic qualifications, a level head is more important than 'A' levels.

If you've already had work experience, so much the better. Maturity is invaluable. You'll need to be an individual. Strong yet flexible. Single-minded yet open-minded. Able to think for yourself yet obey orders. To take all things into consideration and yet make on-the-spot decisions.

We really need men and women from every section of the community, who can get on with people and who feel they

"Its not all about nicking people"

could meet the challenge of looking after ten million Londoners.

A policeman's lot is a hell of a lot. According to a Sunday Times survey, the job has a higher stress-factor than any other.

The rewards however, are unequalled. Pay's good. (We'll not tell you how good until we're sure that isn't the reason you want to join.) The friends you make in the Force will be people you could trust with your life. On occasions, you may have to.

Gradually you decide which way you want your career to develop. Many officers prefer to stay as PCs. You may decide you'd like to take your sergeant's exam. Specialise, and become a Traffic Patrol Officer or Dog Handler or apply

Top right: "Minimum restraint" is applied to a troublemaker.

Below: Inside, the "Hoolivan" bristles with technology. 2 remote cameras, 7 VCRs.

Left: Routine searches on the gate. Metal detectors now installed.

to join the River or Mounted Police. Or apply to become a detective, and in due course perhaps join the Drug Squad, Robbery Squad, Fraud Squad or Special Branch. Whichever path you follow, you'll find there isn't a more satisfying job anywhere. It's not all about nicking people.

Imagine how you'd feel if you'd succeeded in talking someone out of jumping from a fourteenth storey window. Or persuading a kid away from a life of crime who you catch pinching a Mars Bar.

If you'd like to know more about a career in the Met or would like a chat with one of our Careers Advisers who are serving police officers, please fill in the coupon and mail it to us today.

We are looking for men and women who are mature, physically fit and over the age of eighteen and a half. Ideally you'll be at least 172 cms tall if you're a man, 162 cms for a woman, and have 5 'O' levels, although personal qualities are just as important.

To find out more ring: 01-725 4492 (Ansaphone: 01-725 4575) or fill in the coupon or write to: The Recruiting Officer, The Metropolitan Police, Careers Information Centre, Department MD 203, New Scotland Yard, London SW1H 0BG.

Name

Address

Postcode

Age

2 *Advertisement for the Metropolitan Police*

EULOGY DELIVERED BY THE COMMISSIONER
AT THE FUNERAL OF
POLICE CONSTABLE FRANCIS JOSEPH O'NEILL

'All it needs for evil to triumph
is for good men to do nothing'

Francis Joseph O'Neill was a good man. He did not stand aside. He acted. He did so in a way that characterized his police service. It was not done in pursuit of personal ambition, but in the service of others.

He was a dedicated police officer, whose quiet, determined approach to his work epitomizes all that is the strength of the police service; the unarmed constable striving selflessly to uphold the law.

On Saturday, 25 October 1980, Constable O'Neill responded to a call for assistance as he had done many times in the past. All police officers do so in the knowledge of the price which may have to be paid in a world which is becoming ever more violent. Only the few are called upon to pay the price in full.

A police officer must strive to attain a higher standard of duty, must endure a greater degree of self-sacrifice than the ordinary citizen. That is the nature of the British police service and, while it remains so, the confidence and the esteem of the public at large will be secure.

In doing his duty, in making the ultimate sacrifice, Constable O'Neill acted in the finest traditions of the police service. His actions are a testament to the ideals of our policing system, which he staunchly upheld.

At this time our thoughts are principally with the family of Constable O'Neill. No words can adequately describe the grief that they are suffering; no words can sufficiently provide the comfort that they need.

In time,

Out of the darkness there will be light;
Out of the frailty there will be strength; and
Out of the sorrow there will be happiness.

Of that I am certain.

The light, the strength and the happiness for the family will be found in the strong Christian belief that they hold; in the support given by relatives and friends; and in the knowledge that they too are part of a larger family – the police family.

The finest tribute that the Metropolitan Police can pay will be to remember his family. That we will do.

Today relatives, friends and colleagues we pay tribute to Frank.

He gave his life in pursuit of justice; in pursuit of a better life for us all.

Frank O'Neill has not died in vain. His example, his inspiration and his sacrifice will long be remembered. Certainly evil will never triumph while we have officers of his kind.

May he rest in peace.

Sir David McNee, McNEE'S LAW